THE PROCESS TO PRODUCTION

A JOURNEY FROM CALLING TO FULFILLMENT

MARC L. HOUSE

© 2025 Marc L. House

www.vccatl.org

ISBN-13: 9798992206739

The Process to Production

All rights reserved. Printed in the United States of America

All rights reserved. No part of this book may be reproduced or transmitted in any form or by any means, electronic or mechanical, including photocopying, recording, or by any information storage and retrieval system, without permission in writing form the publisher.

Scripture quotations are from the New King James Version®. © 1982 by Thomas Nelson, Inc. Used by permission. All rights reserved.

The Message Bible. Amplified Bible (AMP) Copyright © 1954, 1958, 1962, 1964, 1965, 1987 by The Lockman Foundation.

Scripture quotations marked (MSG) are from *The Message* by Eugne H. Peterson. © 1993, 1994, 1995, 1996, 2000. NavPress Publishing Group.

Scripture quotations marked (NLT) are from *Holy Bible, New Living Translation.* © 1996, 2004, 2007. Tyndale House Publishers, Inc. All rights reserved.

Scripture quotations marked (CEV) are from Contemporary English Version ® Copyright © 1995 American Bible Society. All rights reserved.

Table of Contents

Introduction: The Journey of a Call 1
Chapter 1: The Call 2
Chapter 2: The Character Test 8
Chapter 3: The Waiting Game 17
Chapter 4: The Test of Patience 23
Chapter 5: Facing the Giants 27
Chapter 6: The Breaking Point 36
Chapter 7: The Walk of Submission 42
Chapter 8: Betrayal – A Catalyst for Growth and Redemption 47
Chapter 9: The People Test – Loving Difficult People Without Losing Yourself ... 51
Chapter 10: Rejected Purpose 62
Chapter 11: Frustrated Future 69
Chapter 12: The Power of the Anointing 75
Chapter 13: Called to Serve 84
Chapter 14: Called to Pray 93
Chapter 15: Surviving Assassination Attempts 100
Chapter 16: Becoming a Living Epistle 105
Chapter 17: Life on Stage 110
Chapter 18: The Production Stage 116
Chapter 19: Faithful to the Call 120
Chapter 20: Congratulations 125

Introduction
The Journey of a Call

God's Call to ministry is the beginning of a life-altering journey. It is about the destination and the process—how God shapes, refines, and prepares us for His purposes.

Real ministry involves your entire person, your family, and your resources. Nothing about ministry is part-time. Everything about you lends some reference to your calling. Even your profession or secular employment has some element of training and development of God's calling on our lives. We often miss the fact that your job is also a type of mission field.

We need preparation to function as skilled craftsmen with an assignment, not a shade tree day laborer who imitates the authentic, having the outfit and the tools but no knowledge and skill.

In this journey, you will face challenges, tests, and seasons of waiting, but each step is part of God's intentional plan to mold you into the vessel He needs for His purpose. This book will guide you through the stages from calling to production, emphasizing that the process is just as necessary as the fulfillment.

Chapter 1
The Call

Scripture:

"Before I formed you in the womb I knew you, before you were born I set you apart; I appointed you as a prophet to the nations." (Jeremiah 1:5)

Every believer's journey in ministry begins with a call—a divine summons from God to step into His purpose. This Call is deeply personal and uniquely tailored to the individual, often far beyond what we could imagine for ourselves. Throughout Scripture, God's Call demonstrates that He chooses ordinary, imperfect people to fulfill extraordinary purposes, revealing His power and glory through their lives.

Jeremiah 1:5 reminds us that God's calling is not accidental or random. Before we were even born, God had a plan for our lives. He knows our weaknesses, strengths, hangups, and potential and calls us according to His foreknowledge and divine purpose. Jeremiah's response to God's Call reveals the weight of such a responsibility. When God told Jeremiah that He had appointed him as a prophet to the nations, Jeremiah hesitated, saying, *"Ah, Sovereign Lord, I do not know how to speak; I am too young"* (Jeremiah 1:6). Like many of us, Jeremiah doubted his ability to fulfill the Call. We usually answer from our perceived failures and flaws.

But God reassured him:

"Do not say, 'I am too young.' You must go to everyone I send you to and say whatever I command you. Do not be afraid of them, for I am with you and will rescue you" (Jeremiah 1:7-8).

This passage shows us that God's Call is specific to the person He is calling. He has called you, not your circle. God equips those He calls, overcoming their weaknesses. Our inadequacies don't limit our use by God; our lack of humility does.

God's presence ensures success, even in fear or inadequacy. You can't do a God-sized job with the God who called you. Jesus said, "Without me, you can do nothing."

Your calling is rooted in God's knowledge of you. He sees what you cannot see and calls you not based on who you are now but on who He has created you to be.

In Exodus 3, we find Moses, a shepherd tending the flock of his father-in-law, Jethro. Though Moses had once been a prince in Egypt, his current life was far from glamorous. Yet God chose this moment in Moses' ordinary routine to call him into an extraordinary purpose.

At the burning bush, God spoke:

"So now, go. I am sending you to Pharaoh to bring my people, the Israelites, out of Egypt." (Exodus 3:10)

Moses, like Jeremiah, responded with doubt:

"Who am I that I should go to Pharaoh and bring the Israelites out of Egypt?" (Exodus 3:11)

God replied:

"I will be with you." (Exodus 3:12)

The Call of Moses teaches us several key principles that are relevant today.

God calls in the ordinary; Moses was simply tending sheep when God called him. Often, God meets us in the everyday moments of life to reveal His extraordinary plans.

God Chose the Reluctant, and Moses felt unqualified, pointing out his lack of eloquence (Exodus 4:10). Yet God assured him that He would speak through him.

God's Power Is Made Perfect in Weakness Moses' limitations did not hinder God's plan; instead, they highlighted God's strength and provision.

God calls us not because we are extraordinary but because He is. He uses our weaknesses to display His power.

Throughout Scripture, God repeatedly calls imperfect people to accomplish His perfect will. This pattern demonstrates that His work in us is not about our abilities but about His glory.

- **Abraham:** Called to be the Father of nations despite his old age and moments of doubt (Genesis 12).

- **David:** Anointed as king while still a shepherd boy, despite his later failures and moral lapses (1 Samuel 16).

- **Paul:** A former persecutor of Christians, transformed into one of the greatest apostles (Acts 9).

God's pattern of calling flawed individuals serves to encourage us. He does not require perfection but rather a willingness to obey. As Paul writes:

"But God chose the foolish things of the world to shame the wise; God chose the weak things of the world to shame the strong." (1 Corinthians 1:27)

Your imperfections do not disqualify you from God's Call. Instead, they allow His grace to shine through your life.

The Call is to the one marked off for the master's use. We don't select our service; God does. The kingdom of God is not a grab bag or Job fair of open position because God is desperate. Our pliable nature toward God opens us to an unexplainable avenue of grace. The psalmist declared in the 37th chapter that you should delight yourself in the Lord and that he will give you the desires of your heart.

God's calling is always tied to His greater purpose. Ephesians 4:11-12 explains that God appoints people to ministry for the building up of the Body of Christ:

"So Christ himself gave the apostles, the prophets, the evangelists, the pastors, and teachers, to equip his people for works of service, so that the body of Christ may be built up."

Your calling is not about personal glory or achievement but serving others and glorifying God. When we embrace our calling, we become vessels through God's kingdom, which is advanced on earth. When God calls, it's not just about assigning a task; it's about transforming a life. The Call of

God often redefines how we see ourselves, challenges how we live, and shifts the direction of our lives.

When God calls a person, it is never insignificant or ordinary. His calling is an invitation to partner with Him in His divine mission, to be part of something eternal and life changing. It is an affirmation that your life matters to God, not just for who you are but for the impact He desires to make through you.

The Call of God is far above average because it originates from a perfect, sovereign Creator with a specific plan for your life. To be called by God means that you are not forgotten, overlooked, or random; instead, you are chosen, appointed, and sent for a purpose that transcends your understanding.

Say Yes to God. Both Jeremiah and Moses initially hesitated, but they ultimately submitted to God's Call. Saying "yes" to God opens the door to His purpose in your life. God can't use a part-time Yes. Give God a fresh yes.

Trust His Provision; God equips those He calls. He promises His presence and provision, as He did with Jeremiah (*"I have put my words in your mouth"* – Jeremiah 1:9) and Moses (*"I will help you speak and will teach you what to say"* – Exodus 4:12).

Embrace your weakness and acknowledge that your calling is not about your strength but about God's power working through you.

God's calling is deeply personal, specific, and intentional. He sees beyond your flaws and uses the ordinary and imperfect to accomplish the extraordinary. Like Jeremiah, Moses, and countless others, you are called for a purpose greater than yourself. Trust God, embrace His Call, and allow Him to work through you to fulfill His divine plan.

Prayer

Lord, thank you for calling me even in my imperfection. I trust that your plans for me are good and will equip me for every step of the journey. Help me to surrender to your purpose and walk boldly in the calling You have placed on my life. In Jesus' name, amen.

Chapter 2
The Character Test

Character is the foundation of every calling. While gifts and talents may open doors, the character determines whether you can sustain the calling God has placed on your life. The Greek word for "character" is χαρακτήρ (*charaktér*), which refers to something engraved or stamped, indicating the true nature of a thing. Just as a coin bears the image of its maker, so our lives bear the imprint of our Creator.

The character test is a process God uses to shape us into vessels fit for His purposes. During these tests, God exposes areas of weakness, develops humility, and instills integrity. Throughout Scripture, we see how God tests and refines His people, not to destroy them, but to prepare them for the extraordinary tasks He has called them to accomplish.

But the Lord said to Samuel, 'Do not consider his appearance or height, for I have rejected him. The Lord does not look at the things people look at. People look at the outward appearance, but the Lord looks at the heart.'" (1 Samuel 16:7)

The journey of fulfilling God's Call always includes a season of character testing. This phase is not a punishment but a refining process where God works on the inner man, molding and shaping us to reflect His heart. While the world values external appearances, achievements, and skills, God places the highest value on the condition of our hearts. The character test ensures that we not only accomplish what God has called us to do but that we do it with grace his way.

God isn't concerned with the number of your followers, influence, or gift; it's all a matter of the heart.

In 1 Samuel 16, God sends Samuel to anoint the next king of Israel. Samuel naturally assumes that Eliab, Jesse's oldest son, is the chosen one based on his appearance and stature. But God reveals an important principle: *"People look at the outward appearance, but the Lord looks at the heart"* (1 Samuel 16:7). This profound statement highlights how God's priorities differ from ours. People can look right and still be wrong.

David, the younger son, was tending to sheep when Samuel arrived. By human standards, he seemed the least likely choice for a king. He was the runt of his family and was voted least likely to succeed, yet David's heart set him apart. God even called him a man after my own heart. His humility, faith, and trust in God made him the chosen vessel for this monumental calling.

God often tests and refines our character in private before promoting us in public. The heart must be prepared before the task can be accomplished. Without proper preparation, we tend to lean towards whatever appears to be popular and accepted as successful, never fulfilling our tailor-made calling in the kingdom, rendering the kingdom useless and ineffective, fostered in illegitimacy, and susceptible to major errors because we didn't stay in our lane.

The Refining Process is where the school of Character begins to take shape.

God shapes character through teaching and testing. These seasons are not a walk in the park, but they are essential. In the same way that gold is refined by fire, our character is refined by challenges, trials, and the stretching of our faith.

God uses His Word, the Holy Spirit, and life experiences to teach us His ways. Through Scripture, we learn the importance of humility, integrity, and obedience.

Humility was a core class Jesus taught. He said that the greatest in the kingdom is the one who humbles himself (Matthew 23:12). Humility allows us to depend entirely on God, recognizing that our strength and success come from Him.

The Greek word for humility is **ταπεινοφροσύνη** (*tapeinophrosune*n), meaning a lowliness of mind or an absence of pride. Humility is essential for anyone called by God. Without it, we risk falling into pride and self-reliance, which can derail the calling God has placed on our lives.

Humility is the foundation of godly character. It acknowledges that everything we have and accomplish comes from God. We didn't or couldn't do this without God. Pride often leads to a fall, but humility opens the door to God's favor and guidance. Philippians 2:5-8 teaches us that Jesus humbled Himself, even to the point of death on the cross. His humility brought salvation to the world and demonstrated the power of submission to God's will.

David exemplified humility throughout his life. Even after being anointed King, he returned to tending sheep, faithfully serving in what seemed mundane. Despite knowing he was to replace Saul, David submitted to his authority in Saul's court.

In contrast, Saul failed the humility test. When confronted with his disobedience, Saul blamed others instead of taking responsibility (1 Samuel 15:20-21). His pride and refusal to submit to God's authority led to his downfall.

Integrity lessons are discovered in Proverbs 10:9, which declares, *"Whoever walks in integrity walks securely."* Integrity means doing what is right even when no one is watching, living a life in step with God's truth. Integrity ensures that we live consistently with God's Word. It builds trust with others and honors God.

David demonstrated integrity by sparing Saul's life in the cave, even when it would have been convenient or justified to harm God's anointed (1 Samuel 24:10). Integrity will often cause you to give up your rights to God. In some situations, you have every right to be upset, angry, and retaliate, but you give up your rights for God to handle it.

The Hebrew word for integrity is תָּם(*tam*), meaning completeness, innocence, or moral uprightness. Integrity is the ability to remain faithful to God's standards, even when inconvenient or costly.

Joseph's life is a profound example of integrity in the face of temptation. Sold into slavery by his brothers and later falsely accused by Potiphar's wife, Joseph could have compromised his values to escape hardship. Instead, he chose to honor God, even when it cost him his freedom (Genesis 39:7-9).

God uses the character test to refine our integrity, ensuring we can be trusted with His purposes and people. Psalm 26:1 says, *"Vindicate me, Lord, for I have led a blameless life; I have trusted in the Lord and have not faltered."*

The fundamentals of Obedience we glean from what Samuel told Saul, *"To obey is better than sacrifice"* (1 Samuel 15:22).

Obedience demonstrates our trust in God's wisdom and sovereignty, even when we don't fully understand His why. Obedience is the ultimate test of faith. It requires us to trust God's plan over our desires or understanding.

When God asked Abraham to sacrifice Isaac, Abraham obeyed without hesitation. His obedience revealed his trust in God, and God provided a ram as a substitute (Genesis 22). Every act of obedience comes with a reward.

The Greek word for obedience is ὑπακοή (*hypakoé*), meaning to listen attentively and submit to authority. Obedience is a hallmark of godly character and a critical life test in the refining process.

Moses' life demonstrates the importance of obedience. When God called him from the burning bush to lead the Israelites out of Egypt, Moses initially resisted, offering excuses about his inadequacies (Exodus 3:11-13). Yet, Moses ultimately obeyed, and God used him mightily.

Obedience often requires stepping outside our comfort zones and trusting God with the unknown. It's not enough to know what God wants us to do; we must act on it. James 1:22 reminds us to be doers of the Word, not just hearers.

This test often involves discomfort, delay, and moments of doubt. It exposes areas where we need growth, grooming, and pruning. However, these tests are necessary for growth and preparation. Proverbs 17:3 says, *"The crucible for silver and the furnace for gold, but the Lord tests the heart."*

These moments of revelation are opportunities for repentance and growth. Psalm 139:23-24 says:

"Search me, God, and know my heart; test me and know my anxious thoughts. See if there is any offensive way in me and lead me in the way everlasting."

God uses character tests to prepare us for the weight of our calling. Luke 16:10 teaches, *"Whoever can be trusted with very little can also be trusted with much."* If we cannot handle small responsibilities with integrity and humility, we will not be ready for larger ones.

God allows trials to test the lessons we've learned and to strengthen our faith. James 1:2-4 encourages us to embrace these moments:

"Consider it pure joy, my brothers and sisters, whenever you face trials of many kinds because you know that testing your faith produces perseverance. Let perseverance finish

its work so you may be mature and complete, not lacking anything."

Before he became king, David endured years of being hunted by Saul. Despite opportunities to kill Saul and claim the throne, David trusted God's timing and acted with integrity (1 Samuel 24).

Betrayed by his brothers and imprisoned unjustly, Joseph's character was tested repeatedly. Yet he remained faithful to God, which prepared him to lead and save Egypt during the famine (Genesis 50:20).

Amid immense suffering and loss, Job's unwavering faith and refusal to curse God were revealed in his character (Job 1:21). (Job 1:21).

God cannot use a person for His glory unless their character aligns with his will. God won't lower his standards just to get more followers. Pride, dishonesty, and rebellion hinder His work and damage meaningful relationships.

We have to keep trusting God when our character is being stretched.

The refining process is not an overnight event. It often feels uncomfortable, even painful, as God stretches us beyond what we think we can endure. However, these moments are opportunities to grow and draw closer to God.

Proverbs 3:5-6: *"Trust in the Lord with all your heart and lean not on your understanding; in all your ways submit to Him, and He will make your paths straight."*

Isaiah 64:8: *"Yet you, Lord, are our Father. We are the clay, and you are the potter; we are all the work of your hand."*

God is shaping us like clay in the hands of a potter. While we may not understand the process, we can trust that He is forming us into vessels fit for His purpose.

When we allow God to shape our character, we become equipped to handle the pressure of His calling on our lives. David's years of refining prepared him to be a king after God's own heart (Acts 13:22). Joseph's testing prepared him to save nations. What are you being prepared for?

Passing the character test brings maturity, wisdom, and an anointing within God's will. It also opens the door for more incredible blessings and responsibility in His kingdom.

James 1:12: *"Blessed is the one who perseveres under trial because, having stood the test, that person will receive the crown of life that the Lord has promised to those who love Him."*

The character test is a necessary part of every believer's journey. God is more interested in who we are becoming than in our actions. He values humility, integrity, and obedience above talent or ability. When we trust Him in the refining process, He prepares us for the fullness of His calling.

God is not looking for perfection; He is looking for hearts that are surrendered to Him, willing to be shaped and refined. When we embrace the process, we become vessels fit for His glory, bearing His character and reflecting His nature to the world.

Prayer

Lord, search my heart and refine my character. Please help me to walk in humility, integrity, and obedience. Teach me to trust You in every test, knowing You are shaping me for Your purpose. Strengthen my faith and make me a vessel for Your glory. In Jesus' name, amen.

Chapter 3
The Waiting Game

"Wait for the Lord; be strong, and let your heart take courage; wait for the Lord!" (Psalm 27:14)

Waiting on God and waiting in God is one of the most unique aspects of the Christian journey. It's not about passively passing the time but about actively trusting God, syncing your heart with His will, and preparing for the fulfillment of His promises for your life. However, one of the most significant challenges during a waiting season is avoiding distractions and resisting the urge to move in haste.

The Bible reminds us in **Isaiah 52:12**:

"But you will not leave in haste or go in flight; for the Lord will go before you, the God of Israel will be your rear guard."

This verse reminds us that God's timing is perfect, and moving prematurely can lead to unnecessary consequences. When we wait patiently and avoid impulsive decisions, we allow God to work out every detail for our good and His glory.

Moving in haste is a temptation during waiting seasons because impatience and pressure often push us to "help God along" in fulfilling His promises. But as Isaiah 52:12 teaches, we don't have to rush ahead because God has already gone before us. Trusting Him means believing He is preparing the way and protecting us from behind.

Abraham and Sarah moved in haste when they tried to fulfill God's promise of a son through Hagar (Genesis 16:1-4). Their impatience caused conflict and consequences that affected generations. Waiting on God's timing would have brought peace and clarity.

When we are tempted to move too quickly, follow these three steps pause, pray, and seek counsel from your pastor and God will confirm your moves. Proverbs 19:2 warns, *"Desire without knowledge is not good—how much more will hasty feet miss the way!"*

A waiting believer deeply trusts that God's timing is perfect.

Trust means believing that delays are not denials but divine strategies for preparation.

Joseph trusted God through slavery and imprisonment, knowing that God's plan for his life would come to pass at the right time.

Faithfulness in small, daily tasks shows God our readiness for greater responsibilities. Luke 16:10 teaches *He that is faithful in that which is least is faithful also in much: and he that is unjust in the least is unjust also in much.*

Elijah patiently waited by the brook as God provided for him through ravens (1 Kings 17:2-6). Even when the brook dried up, Elijah trusted God's timing for his next move. We don't move until God speaks. Dry brooks are not an excuse to evacuate.

Hope is the anchor that keeps believers grounded during waiting seasons. The Hebrew word for hope תִּקְוָה (*Tikvah*) also means "a rope" or "cord," symbolizing something you cling to. I want to admonish you not to let go of the rope and not trust people who have let go of theirs.

Lamentations 3:25 encourages:

"The Lord is good to those whose hope is in Him, to the one who seeks Him."

David held onto hope while waiting to become king, even as he faced persecution from Saul.

Spiritual discipline keeps "waiting" believers focused and strengthened. Prayer, worship, and study of the Word anchor the soul and prevent distractions.

Jesus often withdrew to pray, even during active ministry, modeling the importance of remaining connected to the Father (Luke 5:16).

Avoid distractions at all costs; distractions can derail your progress, especially during a waiting season. The danger in distraction is they normally don't look like distractions when they show up. Distractions often come as unfocused people and unnecessary opportunities. They seem like help, private advice, a listening ear, or even our impatience.

Proverbs 4:25-27 advises:

"Let your eyes look straight ahead; fix your gaze directly before you. Give careful thought to the paths for your feet

and be steadfast in all your ways. Do not turn to the right or the left; keep your foot from evil."

Joseph avoided distractions by staying faithful to God, even when tempted by Potiphar's wife. Distraction often appears to fill a void or answer a need.

Waiting develops spiritual depth and strength. It teaches believers to rely on God and not their understanding.

Waiting provides time to deepen your relationship with God. Psalm 37:7 says:

"Be still before the Lord and wait patiently for Him."

Just as a seed must be nurtured before it grows, waiting prepares you to carry out God's purposes. Isaiah 40:31 promises:

"But those who wait for the Lord shall renew their strength; they shall mount up with wings like eagles; they shall run and not be weary; they shall walk and not faint."

Surround Yourself with Godly Influence: Walk with those who encourage your spiritual growth and challenge you to stay focused on God's promises.

The waiting season is not about idleness but about preparation and growth. When we refuse to move in haste and instead embrace the process, we position ourselves to walk into God's promises with strength, clarity, and readiness.

As Psalm 40:1-2 reminds us:

"I waited patiently for the Lord; He turned to me and heard my cry. He lifted me out of the slimy pit, out of the mud and mire; He set my feet on a rock and gave me a firm place to stand."

God doesn't just work on your circumstances—He is working on you. Trust Him, avoid distractions, and embrace the process of transformation. Waiting in position until promoted is a lesson you will learn one way or the other.

Scripture teaches us in **1 Peter 5:6**, *"Humble yourselves, therefore, under God's mighty hand, that He may lift you in due time." Similarly, Timothy remained faithful in his service alongside Paul, growing in spiritual maturity and readiness before stepping into more significant leadership in the church (1 Timothy 4:12-14).*

These examples remind us that God's promotion comes in His perfect timing, as He refines our character and prepares us for the weight of the calling. Waiting faithfully in the position God has placed you ensure that, when the time comes, you are equipped to fulfill His purpose with excellence and grace. God's timing is perfect, and waiting is never wasted when you remain faithful to His process. Shortcuts might seem like a faster path to the promise, but it often leads to consequences and delays. Remember, God is not only preparing the opportunity for you He is preparing you for the opportunity.

Be encouraged by Paul's words in **Galatians 6:9**, *"Let us not grow weary in doing good, for at the proper time we will reap a harvest if we do not give up."*

Trust that God sees your wait, and in His perfect timing, He will promote you in a way that no human effort or shortcut ever could. Stay steadfast, for His plans for you are worth the wait.

Affirmation Prayer

Lord, thank You for the waiting season. Teach me to resist the urge to move in haste and to trust Your perfect timing. Help me to avoid distractions and remain focused on Your promises. Prepare my heart and refine my character so I may walk into the fullness of Your plans with strength and confidence. In Jesus name, amen.

Chapter 4
The Test of Patience

But let patience have its perfect work, that you may be perfect and complete, lacking nothing (James 1:4)

Patience is one of the most valuable virtues to cultivate, yet it is central to walking in agreement with God's will.

The Greek word for patience μακροθυμία (*makrothumia*) translates to "long-suffering" or "endurance." It signifies the ability to remain steadfast under trial, to trust God's timing, and to endure without complaint. God often uses delays, detours, and obstacles to test and grow our patience.

The story of Joseph is a powerful example of enduring delays and detours while remaining faithful to God. Joseph was just a teenager when God gave him dreams of greatness, showing that he would one day rule over his family (Genesis 37:5-11). However, his journey to fulfillment was far from straightforward.

Joseph's brothers, consumed with jealousy, sold him into slavery in Egypt. This betrayal marked the beginning of a long and arduous season. Despite the injustice, Joseph did not abandon his faith in God. Instead, he worked diligently in Potiphar's house, earning favor and success (Genesis 39:2-6).

Just when things seemed to improve, Joseph was falsely accused by Potiphar's wife and thrown into prison (Genesis 39:11-20). Once again, Joseph could have become bitter or given up, but he remained faithful. In the prison, he served others, interpreting dreams and waiting on God's timing (Genesis 40:1-23).

After interpreting the dreams of Pharaoh's cupbearer and baker, Joseph remained in prison for two more years before being remembered and brought before Pharaoh (Genesis 41:1). Finally, at the age of thirty, Joseph was promoted to second-in-command in Egypt, fulfilling the dreams God had given him years earlier (Genesis 41:39-46).

Joseph's life teaches us that delays are not denials. God used each detour to shape Joseph's character, prepare him for leadership, and position him to save his family and an entire nation during a famine.

Delays are not a sign of God's absence but His intentional process. The waiting period is where God refines our character.

Patience grows when we endure trials with faith. Romans 5:3-4 reminds us:

"We also glory in our sufferings because we know that suffering produces perseverance; perseverance, character; and character, hope."

When faced with delays, it's easy to feel discouraged or tempted to give up, however, how we respond to waiting shapes our journey toward fulfilling God's promises.

Avoid Bitterness and Complaining

Philippians 2:14-15 teaches:

"Do everything without grumbling or arguing, so that you may become blameless and pure, 'children of God without fault in a warped and crooked generation.'"

The global pandemic of COVID-19 was a profound reminder of the importance of patience. Entire nations were forced into lockdowns, plans were delayed, and life as we knew it stopped. During this time, many were challenged to wait on God in new ways, learning to trust Him amidst uncertainty.

Many people faced delayed dreams, canceled plans, and financial struggles. Yet, the season reminded us of God's sovereignty and the need to seek Him above all else (Matthew 6:33).

We saw growth during patience, and for many, the pause created opportunities for spiritual growth, family reconnection, and reevaluating priorities.

God's Provision in the Delay: God provided manna in the wilderness and sustained His people through unforeseen challenges (Exodus 16:4).

COVID-19 taught the world that waiting is not passive but an opportunity to grow in trust, creativity, and dependence on God.

While patience develops, rejoice in small wins and celebrate progress, no matter how small. 1 Thessalonians 5:18 reminds us to give thanks in all circumstances.

Keep a God did it Journal: Write down how God has been faithful. Reflecting on His goodness strengthens hope for the future.

The test of patience is a critical part of the process to fulfilling God's Call. Waiting is not wasted; it is a season of preparation, growth, and deepening trust in God. Joseph's life and lessons from recent global events remind us that God's plans are always worth the wait.

Isaiah 30:18 beautifully summarizes this truth:

"Yet the Lord longs to be gracious to you; therefore, He will rise to show you compassion. For the Lord is a God of justice. Blessed are all who wait for Him!"

Patience isn't just about waiting—it's about how you wait. Trust God's timing, avoid discouragement, and remember that He works all things together for your good and His glory (Romans 8:28).

Affirmation Prayer:

Lord, thank You for the gift of patience. Help me to trust Your timing and remain steadfast in the face of delays. Teach me to embrace the waiting season as an opportunity for growth and preparation. I surrender my plans to You, knowing that Your ways are higher and Your timing is perfect. In Jesus' name, In Jesus' name, Amen.

Chapter 5
Facing the Giants

"The Lord who rescued me from the paw of the lion and the paw of the bear will rescue me from the hand of this Philistine." (1 Samuel 17:37)

Every calling will encounter resistance. Whether external opposition like Goliath or internal struggles such as fear, insecurity, or doubt, giants stand in the way of God's plans for our lives. These challenges are not random; they are intentional moments in God's process to develop us, strengthen our faith, and prepare us for more significant victories. Facing giants is a defining aspect of fulfilling your divine assignment.

The word "giant" refers to the physical stature of someone like Goliath and any significant obstacle that seems impossible. The Hebrew term for giants, Nephilim, implies something towering and intimidating (Genesis 6:4). Giants in our lives can be external challenges—opposition from people, systems, or circumstances—or internal struggles, like fear, doubt, and insecurity that hinder us from walking in faith.

Giants are often revealed when we step into God's calling, and their presence is a sign that God is preparing us for something significant. The question is not whether we will face giants but how we will respond when they appear.

The account of David and Goliath in 1 Samuel 17 is one of the most well-known examples of overcoming seemingly impossible challenges.

A Philistine warrior, Goliath stood over nine feet tall, taunting the Israelite army for forty days. His size, strength, and confidence struck fear into Saul's army, causing them to retreat in paralysis (1 Samuel 17:4-11). Goliath represents external opposition—people or situations that challenge our faith, intimidate us, or oppose God's purpose.

David, the young son of Jesse, was not even part of the army but had been sent to deliver food to his brothers. Despite his youth and lack of military experience, David's faith in God was unwavering and unshakable. While others focused on Goliath's size, David focused on God's power. Davids's battle wasn't personal it was purposeful. David was a man fighting a giant who threatened a nation. The Call often winds up fighting giants for others.

David declared:

"You come against me with sword and spear and javelin, but I come against you in the name of the Lord Almighty, the God of the armies of Israel, whom you have defied." (1 Samuel 17:45)

Armed with only a sling, five smooth stones, and no backup. You may fight by yourself, but you are never alone. David defeated Goliath with a single shot, proving that God's power is greater than any earthly weapon (1 Samuel 17:49-50). David's victory was not as much about his skill but about his trust in God's strength. His faith enabled him to conquer what others feared. A giant killer is someone with skill or courage and a mindset rooted in faith, resilience, and unmovable trust in God. David's victory over Goliath was not merely a physical battle but a testament to his spiritual and mental strength. To face and defeat giants, you must possess the mindset of a giant killer—a mindset that overcomes fear, rejects discouragement, and stands firm in the promises of God, even when standing alone.

Giant killers focus on the size of their God, not the size of their opposition.

A giant killer knows their strength comes from God. While others saw Goliath's size and strength as obstacles, David saw an opportunity for God to demonstrate His power. His faith allowed him to step forward when others hesitated.

When David volunteered to fight Goliath, he stood alone. No one encouraged him; in fact, many discouraged him. Saul doubted his ability, saying:

"You are not able to go out against this Philistine and fight him; you are only a young man, and he has been a warrior from his youth." (1 Samuel 17:33)

Even David's brothers mocked him. His eldest brother, Eliab, accused him of arrogance and seeking attention, saying:

"Why have you come down here? And with whom did you leave those few sheep in the wilderness? I know how

conceited you are and how wicked your heart is; you came down only to watch the battle." (1 Samuel 17:28)

Despite their criticism, David remained focused on his mission. He refused to be deterred by their remarks or discouraged by their lack of support. Their lack of support doesn't cancel God's help. A giant killer is willing to stand alone, knowing God is with them.

David had every reason to be distracted—mocked by his brothers, the fear of the Israelite army, and Goliath's overwhelming size and strength. Yet he ignored the noise and focused on the task at hand.

David's response to Eliab's criticism was simple and direct:

"Now, what have I done?" said David. "Can't I even speak?" He then turned away to someone else and brought up the same matter." (1 Samuel 17:29-30)

Rather than engage in pointless arguments or be sidetracked by negativity, David stayed focused on his purpose.

Giant killers know how to ignore distractions and focus on what God has called them to do.

One modern example of facing and defeating giants comes from the world of sports. Michael Oher, a former NFL player whose life inspired the movie *The Blind Side*, overcame incredible odds to fulfill his calling.

Others faced "giants" from a young age. Born into poverty and homelessness, he grew up in an environment filled with instability and a lack of resources. These external giants seemed impossible as he navigated life without essential support or guidance. Internally, Oher battled feelings of inadequacy, rejection, and uncertainty about his future.

Despite these challenges, Oher found support through a Christian family who believed in

his potential. With their encouragement and determination, he embraced his talent in football. Against all odds, he became an NFL player, earning accolades and inspiring millions with his story.

Michael Oher's journey reflects the principles of faith, perseverance, and overcoming giants:

• **Focus on Strength, Not Obstacles**: Like David, Oher relied on his unique abilities and trusted the process to improve his skills.

• **Reject Discouragement**: Oher ignored those who doubted his abilities and focused on the opportunities God placed in his path.

• **Give Glory to God:** Oher acknowledges the role of faith in his journey, attributing his success to God's guidance and the people He placed in his life.

Oher's story reminds us that modern giants—poverty, insecurity, and societal barriers—can be defeated through faith, hard work, and perseverance.

Before you can face your giants, you must identify them. Giants can take many forms, including:

1. External Giants:

- Opposition: Criticism, rejection, or active resistance from others.
- Circumstances: Financial difficulties, health challenges, or systemic barriers.
- Delays: Obstacles that seem to prevent progress or fulfillment of the Call.

2. Internal Giants:

- Fear: Anxiety about failure or inadequacy.
- Insecurity: Feeling unworthy or incapable of fulfilling your calling.
- Doubt: Questioning God's plan or promises.

To identify giants in your life, ask yourself:

• What is causing me to feel overwhelmed or paralyzed?

• What voices of discouragement am I listening to?

• What excuses or fears are keeping me from moving forward?

The Israelite army saw Goliath as unbeatable, but David saw him as an uncircumcised Philistine defying the armies of the living God. His perspective was rooted in faith, not fear. He said:

"Who is this uncircumcised Philistine that he should defy the armies of the living God?" (1 Samuel 17:26)

David's mindset allowed him to see Goliath not as a giant but as an enemy already defeated by God. This faith-filled perspective gave him the courage to step onto the battlefield.

A giant killer views challenges through the lens of God's promises, not their limitations.

David's confidence came from his past experiences with God. He remembered how God had delivered him from the lion and the bear while tending his Father's sheep. These past victories assured him that God would also deliver him from Goliath.

"The Lord who rescued me from the paw of the lion and the paw of the bear will rescue me from the hand of this Philistine." (1 Samuel 17:37)

A giant killer reflects on how God has been faithful in the past, using those victories as fuel for future battles.

A giant killer relies on God's proven track record of faithfulness.

"The Lord who rescued me from the paw of the lion and the paw of the bear will rescue me from the hand of this Philistine." (1 Samuel 17:37)

David boldly declared his victory before the fight even began:

"This day the Lord will deliver you into my hands, and I'll strike you down and cut off your head." (1 Samuel 17:46)

This declaration was not arrogance; it was faith. David knew God's power would give him victory, and he confidently said it.

A giant killer speaks words of faith, aligning their words with God's promises. Proverbs 18:21 reminds us: *"The tongue has the power of life and death."*

Giants are opportunities for God to demonstrate His power through us. As Paul states in Romans 8:37:

"Nay, in all these things, we are more than conquerors through Him who loved us."

David didn't wear Saul's armor or use his weapons; he used the tools God had already equipped him with—a sling and stones. Trust that God has already given you what you need to face your giant. You have a treasure in you.

The reward for facing your giants is not just the victory itself but the spiritual growth, confidence, and testimony from overcoming. God uses these battles to shape us into the people He has called us to be. Like David, your victory over giants can inspire others and bring glory to God. One man's battle saved a nation. Defeating your giants will save a generation.

Affirmation Prayer

Lord, I thank You for the challenges that stretch my faith and draw me closer to You. Help me to see giants as opportunities for growth and to trust in Your power to overcome. Strengthen my heart to face fear, doubt, and opposition with confidence in Your promises. In Jesus' name, amen.

Chapter 6
The Breaking Point

"My grace is sufficient for you, for my power is made perfect in weakness." (2 Corinthians 12:9)

Before fulfilling your calling or the full manifestation of your gift, there often comes a breaking point—a moment where the weight of the journey feels unbearable, and you're tempted to give up. This breaking point is not a place of defeat but transformation. God uses brokenness to refine, restore, and prepare us for the purpose He has called us to fulfill. In the breaking, He shows us that His strength is made perfect in our weakness.

In 1 Kings 19, we find the prophet Elijah at his breaking point. After a triumphant victory on Mount Carmel, where God answered his prayer with fire and defeated the prophets of Baal (1 Kings 18:36-39), Elijah faced an intense backlash from Jezebel, who vowed to kill him.

Elijah, overwhelmed by fear and exhaustion, fled into the wilderness. He cried out to God:

"I have had enough, Lord. Take my life; I am no better than my ancestors." (1 Kings 19:4)

Elijah's breaking point reveals the toll that spiritual warfare, opposition, and exhaustion can take on even the most faithful servants of God. He was physically tired, emotionally drained, and spiritually discouraged. All of this shows up on the heels of his greatest victory.

The breaking point often comes when the pressures of life collide with our human limitations.

Instead of rebuking Elijah for his despair, God ministered to him with compassion. He sent an angel to provide food and water, saying:

"Get up and eat, for the journey is too much for you." (1 Kings 19:7)

After Elijah rested and ate, God led him to Mount Horeb, where He revealed Himself in a gentle whisper (1 Kings 19:11-12). This encounter reminded Elijah that God's power and presence are not always demonstrated dramatically but in quiet reassurance.

God meets us at our breaking points, not with condemnation but with provision, rest, and his gentle presence.

One of Jesus' closest disciples, Peter, also faced a breaking point. In Luke 22:31-34, Jesus warns Peter:

"Simon, Simon, Satan has asked to sift all of you as wheat. But I have prayed for you, Simon, that your faith may not fail. And when you have turned back, strengthen your brothers."

The Greek word for "sift" is σνιάζω (*siniazo*), meaning shaking violently or separating. Jesus warned Peter that Satan desired to test him, to expose any weakness in his faith. Peter, confident in his loyalty, replied:

"Lord, I am ready to go with you to prison and death." (Luke 22:33)

Yet Jesus knew Peter's breaking point was coming. He prophesied:

"Before the rooster crows today, you will deny three times that you know me." (Luke 22:34)

When Peter later denied Jesus, he experienced the depth of his weakness and failure. This moment of brokenness shattered his pride and self-reliance.

Despite Peter's denial, Jesus prayed for him, ensuring his faith would endure. After His resurrection, Jesus restored Peter, reaffirming his calling and commissioning him to "feed my sheep" (John 21:15-17).

The breaking point reveals our need for God's grace and is often the catalyst for transformation and restoration.

What Happens in a Mind That Wants to Quit?

At the breaking point, the mind becomes overwhelmed by a flood of emotions and thoughts that can make quitting seem like the only option. These include:

1. **Fear:** The overwhelming sense of failure or the task's impossibility.

2. **Exhaustion:** Physical, emotional, and spiritual fatigue that clouds judgment.

3. **Self-Doubt:** Questioning your worth, ability, or calling.

4. **Isolation:** Feeling abandoned or misunderstood.

At the breaking point, one of the most important things to do is remember *why* you began the journey in the first place. Burnout doesn't happen because of the demands of the work itself—it happens when we lose sight of the purpose behind what we're doing. When Elijah wanted to give up, he had momentarily forgotten the reason for his calling: to glorify God and lead His people back to Him. Similarly, Peter's denial of Jesus was a momentary lapse in remembering his deep love for Christ and the mission he was called to. Hebrews 12:2 reminds us to fix our eyes on Jesus, *"the pioneer and perfecter of faith. For the joy set before Him, He endured the cross, scorning its shame, and sat down at the right hand of the throne of God."* Keeping the "why" in front of you—glorifying God, serving others, or fulfilling a divine purpose—fuels perseverance and reignites passion. When you remember why you started, the weight of the work becomes lighter, and God's grace carries you through.

In overwhelming pressure and exhaustion, the most powerful response is to surrender fully to God. Surrender is not giving up; it is giving *over*—releasing control and trusting God to carry what we cannot. When Elijah cried out, *"I have had enough, Lord. Take my life"* (1 Kings 19:4), he was at his breaking point, yet even in his despair, he turned to God. Similarly, Jesus, overwhelmed in the Garden of Gethsemane, prayed, *"Father, if you are willing, take this cup from me; yet not my will, but yours be done"* (Luke 22:42). This act of surrender opens the door for God's strength to meet us in our weakness. As Paul reminds us in 2 Corinthians 12:9, God's response to our brokenness is: *"My grace is sufficient for you, for my strength is made perfect in weakness."* When you bring your overwhelmed heart to God, He exchanges your burden for His peace, exhaustion for His sustaining grace, and weakness for His power to carry you forward. Complete surrender allows God to take the weight of your calling and transform your brokenness into a testimony of His faithfulness.

This is How to Endure the Breaking Point Without Quitting

Turn to God in Prayer:

Like Elijah and Peter, bring your fears and failures to God. He hears your cries and offers grace in your weakness.

• *"Cast all your anxiety on Him because He cares for you."* (1 Peter 5:7)

Rest and Recharge:

Sometimes, the most spiritual thing you can do is rest. God ministered to Elijah's physical needs before addressing his spiritual concerns.

Remember God's Promises:

Remind yourself of the calling and promises God has spoken over your life.

• *"Being confident of this, that He who began a good work in you will carry it on to completion until the day of Christ Jesus."* (Philippians 1:6)

Seek God's Perspective:

Let God remind you of His power and faithfulness, as He did with Elijah through the gentle whisper.

Breaking points always Lead to Breakthrough. The breaking point is not the end; it's where God's power meets your weakness. Elijah's breaking point led to a renewed understanding of God's presence and a fresh mission to anoint new leaders (1 Kings 19:15-18). Peter's breaking point led to his transformation into a bold leader of the early church.

Your breaking point is a doorway to more profound dependence on God and greater clarity in your calling. Trust that God is with you, even in your most broken moments, and that He is using this season to prepare you for what lies ahead.

Affirmation Prayer:

Lord, I thank You for meeting me at my breaking point. Help me to surrender my fears, doubts, and weariness to You. Strengthen me with Your grace and remind me that Your power is made perfect in my weakness. I trust that You are using this season to refine and prepare me for the calling You have placed on my life. In Jesus' name, amen.

Chapter 7
The Walk of Submission

"But Jesus answered and said to him, 'Permit it to be so now, for thus it is fitting for us to fulfill all righteousness.' Then he allowed Him. When He had been baptized, Jesus came up immediately from the water; behold, the heavens were opened to Him, and He saw the Spirit of God descending like a dove and alighting upon Him." (Matthew 3:15-16)

Submission is often misunderstood as a position of weakness, but submission is the gateway to elevation in God's kingdom. Jesus, the Son of God, demonstrated this truth when He willingly submitted to being baptized by John the Baptist. Though Jesus knew He was sinless and far greater in stature and purpose than John, He chose to humble Himself and fulfill all righteousness. This submission set the stage for the heavens to open, for God to affirm Him, and for the Spirit to descend upon Him in power.

Submission is not about inferiority; it's about humility

Jesus and John are a Divine Example of Submission

In Matthew 3, Jesus approached John the Baptist at the Jordan River to be baptized. John, recognizing who Jesus was, resisted at first, saying, *"I need to be baptized by You, and are You coming to me?"* (Matthew 3:14). Yet Jesus insisted, saying, *"Permit it to be so now, for thus it is fitting for us to fulfill all righteousness."*

This moment was not about hierarchy but about obedience to God's plan. Jesus' submission to John's baptism demonstrated that even the Son of God was willing to humble Himself to fulfill God's will.

Submission is not about exalting another person but about exalting God's purpose.

As soon as Jesus submitted to baptism, the heavens opened, and God's voice declared, *"This is My beloved Son, in whom I am well pleased"* (Matthew 3:17). This divine endorsement followed an act of humility and submission, not his miracles.

Submission as a Gateway to Elevation

The principle Jesus demonstrated is clear: you cannot rise in God's kingdom until you first humble yourself. My Father, Elder Ronald House, once told me, "Anything that's going high must first go low." The Bible repeatedly affirms this:

- *"Humble yourselves in the sight of the Lord, and He will lift you."* (James 4:10)

- *"Whoever exalts himself will be humbled, and whoever humbles himself will be exalted."* (Matthew 23:12)

Before Jesus began His public ministry, He modeled submission and humility, showing us that these qualities are prerequisites for spiritual promotion.

The Struggle with Submission

Submission is often difficult because it requires us to:

1. **Set aside pride**: Like John, we may feel unworthy, or like others, we may resist submission because it feels beneath us.

2. **Trust God's process**: Submission often comes before clarity or promotion. Jesus had not yet begun His ministry, but He trusted that submission was part of God's preparation.

3. **Align with God's timing**: Submission requires waiting on God's timing, as seen throughout the lives of those God calls.

- **David and Saul:** David submitted to Saul's authority, even though he was already anointed king because he trusted God's timing (1 Samuel 24:6).

- **Moses and Jethro**: Moses submitted to the wisdom of his father-in-law Jethro, even though he was the chosen leader of Israel, demonstrating humility in leadership (Exodus 18:17-24).

Submission Opens the Heavens

When Jesus submitted to John, the heavens opened, and the Spirit descended on Him like a dove. This submission was pivotal for Jesus' ministry, marking the moment The Holy Spirit empowered him.

Submission brings divine affirmation, empowerment, endorsement, and access to God's promises.

As the heavens opened for Jesus, submission can open spiritual doors in your life. When you align yourself with

God's plan and humbly submit to His process, you position yourself for His favor and blessing.

Submission must be embraced like your calling.

Submission begins with understanding and yielding to God's purpose for your life. Pray for clarity and wisdom as you navigate this process.

Acknowledge that God's ways are higher than your own. Be willing to submit to His process, even when it doesn't make sense.

Submission often involves honoring earthly authorities that God has placed in your life, such as mentors, pastors, or leaders.

Remember that submission is not about control but protection within God's plan. Trust that He will exalt you in time (1 Peter 5:6).

Submission as a Process

Submission is not a one-time event but a continuous process that requires daily surrender to God's will. Jesus' example teaches us that submission is a posture of the heart—a willingness to go low so that God can take us higher.

Submission Precedes Promotion: Before Jesus began His ministry, He submitted to John. Before David became king, he submitted to Saul. Before Joseph ruled Egypt, he submitted to prison and servitude.

2. Humility unlocks your heavens; submission invites God's favor, affirmation, and empowerment.

3. God Rewards our obedience; the path of submission leads to spiritual elevation and the fulfillment of God's purpose in your life.

Affirmation Prayer

Lord, teach me the power of submission. Help me to humble myself under Your mighty hand, trusting that in due time, You will lift me. I submit to Your process, even when I don't understand it, knowing that You are working all things for my good and Your glory. Open the heavens over my life as I walk in obedience and surrender to You. In Jesus' name, amen.

Chapter 8
Betrayal – A Catalyst for Growth and Redemption

"For I have received of the Lord that which also I delivered unto you, that the Lord Jesus the same night he was betrayed took bread." 1 Corinthians 11:23

Betrayal cuts deep. It's the unexpected dagger from someone trusted, a friend, a confidant, or even a loved one. The pain of betrayal is so profound because it violates trust, the cornerstone of any meaningful relationship. It leaves us questioning ourselves, others, and often, even God. But while betrayal can break the heart, it can also shape the soul.

At its core, betrayal is an act of selfishness. It is often motivated by greed, envy, or fear—human weaknesses that prioritize personal gain over loyalty and love. What makes betrayal so painful is the intimacy of the relationship it breaks. A stranger cannot betray you; betrayal requires proximity.

Psalm 41:9 captures the sting of such betrayal: *"Even my close friend, someone I trusted, one who shared my bread, has turned against me."* Betrayal hurts deeply because it is personal. It violates our trust, sense of belonging, safety, and identity.

But while we cannot control the actions of others, we can control our response. This truth, though difficult, is empowering. Betrayal need not define us—it can refine us.

No story of betrayal is as iconic as that of Jesus and Judas. Judas Iscariot was one of Jesus' twelve disciples who walked with Him, witnessed His miracles, and heard His teachings. Yet for thirty pieces of silver, Judas betrayed Jesus into the hands of His enemies (Matthew 26:14-16).

What's remarkable about Jesus is His response. Knowing Judas would betray Him at the Last Supper, Jesus still washed his feet (John 13:5-11). He broke bread with him, saying, *"The one who has dipped his hand into the bowl with me will betray me."* (Matthew 26:23). Even in betrayal, Jesus extended grace.

Judas's betrayal didn't derail Jesus' ministry—it fulfilled it. His act of treachery set in motion the events leading to the crucifixion, which brought salvation to the world. Jesus' response to betrayal was not vengeance but purpose. He understood that betrayal could be a steppingstone to a greater mission.

King David, too, knew the sting of betrayal. Ahithophel, a trusted advisor who had sat at David's table, turned against him and joined David's rebellious son, Absalom (2 Samuel 15:12). The betrayal was devastating because it came from someone David had deeply trusted.

David's response was rooted in his faith. In Psalm 55:22, David writes, *"Cast your cares on the Lord, and He will sustain you; He will never let the righteous be shaken."* Though hurt and angered, David trusted God to vindicate him. Ultimately, Ahithophel's betrayal led to his downfall, not David's.

Betrayal often has a boomerang effect, harming the betrayer more than the betrayed. After betraying Jesus, Judas was consumed by guilt. He tried to return the silver, declaring, *"I have sinned by betraying innocent blood."* (Matthew 27:4). When the chief priests rejected him, Judas hanged himself, unable to live with the weight of his actions (Matthew 27:5).

The lesson here is stark: you don't have to carry the burden of someone else's betrayal. Judas's end reminds us that God is the ultimate judge. Vengeance and justice belong to Him (Romans 12:19). Instead of succumbing to the weight of betrayal, we can leave it in God's hands.

When betrayal happens, it's easy to feel powerless. But our response is always within our control. Jesus and David show us that betrayal can be an opportunity to lean into God, trusting Him to turn what was meant for harm into good (Genesis 50:20). Don't fall prey to the mirage of retaliation or revenge in moments like this when we take our eyes off of our calling and put our eyes on paying people back for paying invoked, we lose sight of the mission. We lose sight of our calling. You cannot Respond or repay them for what they did. You needed a Judas to get you to where you're going.

Betrayal has the potential to break us or build us. When we view it through the lens of Scripture, we see that, though painful, betrayal often precedes breakthrough. Jesus' betrayal led to the cross—and, ultimately, the resurrection. David's betrayal by Ahithophel led to his deeper trust in God's sovereignty.

If you've been betrayed, remember: the betrayal is not the end of your story. What others meant for harm, God can use for good. Like Jesus, you can rise above betrayal, trusting that God's plans for you are more significant than any wound inflicted by another.

The art of betrayal may be destructive, but the art of forgiveness and faith is redemptive. Let God take your pain and transform it into something beautiful.

Affirmation Prayer

Father,

I come to You with a heart weighed down by betrayal. I release this pain into Your hands, trusting You to heal and restore me. I declare that this betrayal will not define me—Your love does. Help me to forgive as You have forgiven me and guard my heart against bitterness. I trust you to bring justice in Your perfect way and time. I believe you will use what the enemy meant for harm for my good. Thank You for being my strength, my defender, and my peace. I choose to walk forward in faith, knowing Your plans for me are greater than this hurt.

In Jesus' name, amen.

Chapter 9
The People Test – Loving Difficult People Without Losing Yourself

"By this shall all men know that ye are my disciples if ye have love one to another." John 13:35

Dealing with difficult people is one of the most challenging tests we face in life. Whether toxic, abrasive, or simply hard to love, these individuals often seem placed in our lives to test our patience, character, and faith. But what if these problematic people are also the ones we are called to help, to minister to, or to bless? What if they are part of God's refining process in our own lives?

This test is about maintaining godly character, even when everything in us wants to respond in anger or frustration. It's about not letting the enemy's schemes cause us to hate what we've been sent to heal.

The "people test" occurs when we encounter complex individuals who challenge our faith, patience, and love. These people may criticize, betray, or oppose us, yet we are called to respond with grace and compassion.

"Do not be overcome by evil but overcome evil with good." (Romans 12:21)

This verse reminds us that how we respond to others reflects our character, not theirs. The goal is not just to endure the test but to pass it with a Christlike attitude.

Why We're Tested with Difficult People

Difficult people will expose areas of pride, impatience, or bitterness in us. God uses these interactions to sanctify us, shaping us into His image.

True love is not tested by those who are easy to love but by those who are difficult. God calls us to love as He loves—freely, sacrificially, and without expecting anything in return. *"But I say to you, love your enemies and pray for those who persecute you."* (Matthew 5:44)

The enemy seeks to distract us by turning our hearts against the people we are called to bless. He derails our ministry if he can make us hate or resent them.

Scripture: *"For our struggle is not against flesh and blood, but against the rulers, against the authorities, against the powers of this dark world and against the spiritual forces of evil in the heavenly realms."* (Ephesians 6:12)

Responding to difficult people with godly character requires intentionality and reliance on the Holy Spirit. Here are some key principles:

1. Guard Your Heart

The enemy aims to plant bitterness, anger, or hatred in your heart. Guard against this by keeping your heart rooted in God's love.

Scripture: *"Above all else, guard your heart, for everything you do flows from it."* (Proverbs 4:23)

When dealing with a problematic person, pause and pray. Ask God to protect your heart and fill you with His love.

2. Don't Render Evil for Evil

When someone wrongs us, the natural response is retaliation. But Jesus calls us to a higher standard.

Scripture: *"Do not repay anyone evil for evil. Be careful to do what is right in the eyes of everyone."* (Romans 12:17)

Action: Instead of retaliating, seek to respond with kindness. Speak blessings over those who curse you and pray for those who hurt you.

3. Rely on the Holy Spirit

Loving difficult people is not something we can do with our strength. We need the Holy Spirit to empower us with supernatural patience and love.

Scripture: "But the fruit of the Spirit is love, joy, peace, forbearance, kindness, goodness, faithfulness, gentleness, and self-control." (Galatians 5:22-23)

Action: Pray for the Holy Spirit to produce His fruit in you, especially in conflict or frustration.

4. See the Bigger Picture

Often, difficult people are often hurting themselves, and their behavior reflects their inner struggles. Instead of reacting to their actions, ask God to show you their more profound need.

Scripture: *"Father, forgive them, for they do not know what they are doing."* (Luke 23:34)

Action: Shift your perspective from their behavior to their need for God's healing. Pray for them, asking God to work in their hearts and lives.

Satan's goal is to make you hate what you've been called to help. He wants to turn your focus from ministry to resentment. But you can rise above the offense when you see the spiritual battle at play.

Scripture: *"Be alert and of sober mind. Your enemy, the devil, prowls around like a roaring lion looking for someone to devour."* (1 Peter 5:8)

Stay spiritually vigilant. When you feel frustration rising, remind yourself that your battle is not with the person but with the enemy's attempt to derail you.

Overcoming the People Test

The goal of the people test is not just to survive but to thrive in your mission. Here's how:

1. Pray for Them: Follow Jesus' example by praying for those who challenge you. Prayer softens your heart and invites God into the situation.

2. Bless Them: Speak words of kindness and encouragement. Your actions reflect God's grace even when they don't deserve it.

"Bless those who curse you, pray for those who mistreat you." (Luke 6:28)

3. Trust God for Justice: Leave vengeance in God's hands. Trust Him to deal with wrongs in His way and His time.

"Do not take revenge, my dear friends, but leave room for God's wrath." (Romans 12:19)

4. Focus on Your Mission: Remember that you are called to reflect Christ, not respond kindly. Keep your eyes on the purpose God has given you.

Jesus encountered many difficult people during His ministry. The Pharisees constantly challenged Him, Judas betrayed Him, and Peter denied Him. Yet, Jesus never wavered in His mission or His love for people.

His ultimate example came on the cross. Surrounded by mockers, He prayed, *"Father, forgive them, for they do not know what they are doing."* (Luke 23:34). Jesus passed the people's test by responding with grace, love, and forgiveness, showing us how to do the same.

The people test is not about changing difficult people but changing us. It refines our character, deepens our reliance on God, and strengthens our ability to love like Jesus.

The next time you encounter someone who tests your patience, remember this is not an accident. God has placed you in their life to be a light. Don't let the enemy make you hate what you've been sent to help. With God's grace, you can pass the test and glorify Him in the process.

Often, the very people who test us the most are the ones God sends us to bless or minister to. Maintaining godly character in such moments requires a heart filled with love, a commitment to not render evil for evil, and a perspective rooted in the example of Christ.

But how do we show compassion when our patience is stretched thin? How do we extend grace when we are met with hostility? And how do we stay faithful when the devil tries to make us hate what we've been called to heal?

Compassion is seeing someone's pain or struggle and responding with kindness and love, even when they don't deserve it. It goes beyond mere tolerance; it is the intentional choice to love others as Christ loves us.

Compassion comes from the Latin word *"compati"*, meaning "to suffer with." It is the willingness to enter someone's world, understand their hurt, and respond with care.

"Be kind and compassionate to one another, forgiving each other, just as in Christ God forgave you." (Ephesians 4:32)

Compassion is not just a feeling; it's an action. It's what turns frustration into grace and transforms our response to difficult people from anger to love.

God's love for us is rooted in compassion. He sees our flaws, yet He responds with mercy and grace. We are called to reflect His heart to others.

"The Lord is compassionate and gracious, slow to anger, abounding in love." (Psalm 103:8)

Difficult people often act out of their hurt, insecurity, or brokenness. Compassion allows us to see their pain rather than just their actions.

Jesus didn't focus on their sin or shortcomings when he saw the crowds. Instead, *"He had compassion on them, because they were harassed and helpless, like sheep without a shepherd."* (Matthew 9:36)

Compassion interrupts the Cycle of Retaliation. Instead of escalating conflict, it disarms hostility with love.

The Ultimate Example of Compassion was Jesus. He faced countless difficult people, from the Pharisees who sought to trap Him to the disciples who often misunderstood Him. Yet, He always responded with compassion.

One powerful example is Judas Iscariot. Jesus knew Judas would betray Him, yet He still washed his feet, breaking bread with him at the Last Supper (John 13:1-30). This compassion shows us that we can respond with love even when betrayed.

"Father, forgive them, for they do not know what they are doing." (Luke 23:34)

Even on the cross, Jesus displayed compassion for those who crucified Him. He chose forgiveness over resentment, showing us that compassion is a deliberate choice, not a reaction.

Compassion in Action has Practical Steps for Dealing with Difficult People

1. See Them Through God's Eyes:

Ask God to give you His perspective on the person. Pray to see their potential, not just their flaws.

2. Pause and Respond with Love:

When frustration rises, take a moment to pause and slow the world down before you war with words. Breathe and pray. Ask God to guide your words and actions.

"A gentle answer turns away wrath, but a harsh word stirs up anger." (Proverbs 15:1)

3. Pray for Them:

Prayer is one of the most compassionate things you can do for a difficult person. It not only softens their heart but also changes yours.

Instead of complaining about them, lift them in prayer. Pray for their healing, salvation, and growth.

4. Show Kindness, Even When It's Hard:

Kindness has the power to break down walls. A kind gesture or word can open doors that anger cannot.

"If your enemy is hungry, feed him; if he is thirsty, give him something to drink." (Romans 12:20)

5. Set Healthy Boundaries:

Compassion does not mean enabling bad behavior. Setting boundaries while still loving and praying for the person is okay.

The Enemy's Strategy always turns you against your mission and often uses difficult people to distract and discourage you. His goal is to make us resent the very people we are called to minister to. If he can plant seeds of hatred or bitterness in our hearts, he can derail our mission.

"For we are not unaware of his schemes." (2 Corinthians 2:11)

Instead of falling into this trap, recognize the spiritual battle at play. Ask God for the strength to love, even when it's hard, and to stay focused on your mission.

Love and compassion are transformative forces. They can soften the hardest hearts and heal the deepest wounds. When we respond to difficult people with compassion, we reflect Christ's character and create opportunities for God to work in their lives.

"Above all, love each other deeply, because love covers over a multitude of sins." (1 Peter 4:8)

Passing the Test with Compassion is mandatory for anyone who has been called.

1. Remember Your Own Need for Grace:

We are all recipients of God's compassion. Extending that grace to others becomes easier when we remember how much we've been forgiven.

"Freely you have received; freely give." (Matthew 10:8)

2. Be a Vessel of God's Love:

Difficult people are not in your life by accident. God may have placed you there to be His hands and feet. Ask Him to use you as a vessel of His love and compassion.

Leave Justice to God:

Compassion doesn't mean ignoring wrongdoing. It means trusting God to handle it in His way and His time.

"Do not take revenge, my dear friends, but leave room for God's wrath." (Romans 12:19)

Compassion is the Key to Victory. The people test is not about changing others—it's about changing us. Compassion is the key to passing this test, enabling us to love as Christ loves and to stay faithful to our mission.

The next time you encounter a difficult person, remember this is not just a test of patience—it's a test of love. Let compassion guide your response, and trust God to use your actions to glorify Him and bring healing to those around you.

By embracing compassion, you overcome the people's test and become a powerful instrument of God's grace in a broken world.

Affirmation Prayer

Heavenly Father,

I acknowledge that sometimes I struggle with the words and actions of those who challenge me. Today, I choose to see them through Your eyes, remembering that they are also loved and valued by You. I release any bitterness or offense I hold in my heart, trusting You to heal my wounds and guide my responses with gentleness and wisdom.

I affirm that I am not defined by someone else's behavior. In Christ, I have peace, patience, and the strength to respond in love. Even when others test my patience, I will not be overcome by anger or resentment. Instead, I commit myself to kindness, compassion, and humility.

Lord, fill me with understanding and discernment. Help me to see past the difficulties and into the human hearts behind them. Where there is confusion, let Your truth bring clarity. Where there is tension, let Your Spirit bring calm. I trust You to work in every relationship, and I stand firm, knowing that with You, I can face every challenge with grace. In Jesus' name, amen.

Chapter 10 Rejected Purpose

Key Verse: "And Elisha said, 'As the Lord lives, and as your soul lives, I will not leave you!' So they went down to Bethel." (2 Kings 2:2)

Purpose is a divine thread woven into the fabric of our lives. It connects us to people, places, and assignments that allow us to fulfill our destiny when aligned with God's will. Yet, purpose is not always embraced—it can be misunderstood, delayed, or even rejected by others or us. Purpose is often tied to divine relationships. These are the connections God orchestrates to shape us, challenge us, and prepare us for our destiny. Yet, these relationships often come with tests of loyalty and perseverance. The story of Elijah and Elisha provides a profound lesson about the importance of staying connected and the power of loyalty in fulfilling your God-given purpose.

The Call Requires Connection

Elisha's journey began when Elijah cast his mantle upon him while plowing his field (1 Kings 19:19). This act signified a divine call—a summons to leave his old life and follow Elijah into a prophetic destiny. Elisha immediately responded by leaving work, sacrificing his oxen, and committing himself to serve Elijah.

Elisha's loyalty to Elijah was not merely about obedience; it was about recognizing that his purpose was tied to Elijah. He understood that the Call to follow wasn't just an opportunity but a covenant. Without Elijah, there would be no mantle, no double portion, and no fulfillment of the prophetic legacy he was meant to carry. Remember whose mantle you carry. It's a privilege, not a right.

The Journey of Elisha: Staying in Purpose

The exchange of Elijah and Elisha in 2 Kings 2 illustrates the resolve it takes to walk in purpose. Elisha was called to be Elijah's successor, destined to carry on his prophetic ministry and inherit a double portion of his spirit. However, this journey was challenging. At pivotal moments, Elijah seemingly tried to leave Elisha behind. Throughout their journey, Elijah tested Elisha's resolve by repeatedly asking him to stay behind. At Gilgal, Bethel, and Jericho, Elijah allowed Elisha to stop following. Elisha's response was unwavering each time: *"As the Lord lives, and as your soul lives, I will not leave you."*

Elisha could have interpreted Elijah's insistence as permission to take an easier path. He could have stayed behind and claimed he had been "released" from his commitment. But Elisha saw beyond the surface. He understood that his connection to Elijah was essential for fulfilling his purpose. To leave Elijah would be to abandon the very source of his preparation and inheritance. Mantles don't fall from the sky you can't get a mantle without an MAN/WOMAN.

Gilgal: The Place of Beginnings

Elijah said to Elisha, "Stay here, please, for the Lord has sent me on to Bethel." (2 Kings 2:2)

Gilgal represents a place of beginnings. Here, the Israelites first established themselves in the Promised Land (Joshua 4:19). For Elisha, Gilgal could have been a comfortable stopping point—a place to rest in the assurance of his initial calling. But purpose demands more than beginnings; it requires perseverance.

Elisha responded, "As the Lord lives, and as your soul lives, I will not leave you!" His determination to follow Elijah beyond Gilgal shows that he understood the Call on his life was not to be partially fulfilled. To remain at Gilgal would have been to reject the fullness of his purpose.

Bethel: The Place of Revelation

Bethel was a place of spiritual encounters, known as the location where Jacob saw the ladder reaching to heaven (Genesis 28:12). Elijah again tested Elisha's resolve: "Stay here, please, for the Lord has sent me on to Jericho." (2 Kings 2:4)

At Bethel, Elisha could have chosen to remain in the comfort of revelation, satisfied with his spiritual insight. However, purpose calls us to act on revelation, not merely to sit in its glow. Elisha's refusal to stay behind shows his commitment to pursue purpose, no matter the cost.

Jericho: The Place of Warfare

Jericho symbolizes the place of spiritual battles and breakthroughs, as it was the first city conquered by the Israelites in the Promised Land (Joshua 6). Elijah said,

"Stay here, please, for the Lord has sent me on to the Jordan." (2 Kings 2:6)

Elisha's persistence in following Elijah to Jericho demonstrates his willingness to endure the trials and challenges of fulfilling his purpose. He understood that spiritual inheritance requires faithfulness, even in difficulty. To stop at Jericho would have been to reject the mantle of leadership and the double portion he was destined to receive.

The Jordan: The Place of Transition

Finally, Elisha followed Elijah to the Jordan River, a place of transition and transformation. When Elijah was taken up to heaven in a whirlwind, Elisha cried out, "My father, my father, the chariot of Israel and its horsemen!" (2 Kings 2:12). Only then did he receive Elijah's mantle, signifying the transfer of authority and the fulfillment of his purpose.

The Opportunity Never Outweighs Loyalty

In our pursuit of purpose, we may face moments where opportunities arise that tempt us to abandon our commitments. Elisha's journey reminds us that true purpose is not about seizing every opportunity but about staying faithful to the relationships and assignments God has placed in our lives.

Elisha could have justified leaving Elijah at any point. He could have reasoned that he was called to ministry and didn't need to follow Elijah to the end. But Elisha knew that the mantle—his ultimate purpose—was not just about the calling but about the connection. He needed to stay with Elijah because the fulfillment of his destiny was tied to his loyalty.

The world often values ambition over loyalty, but in God's kingdom, loyalty precedes promotion. Staying connected to the one who called you is not about limiting yourself; it's about honoring the process God has designed for your growth and preparation.

He would have forfeited his divine calling if Elisha stayed behind at Gilgal, Bethel, or Jericho. His story teaches us that purpose is tied to persistence. It often requires us to follow even when the path is unclear, or others might discourage us.

The Reward of Loyalty

Elisha's faithfulness was ultimately rewarded. When Elijah was taken up to heaven in a whirlwind, Elisha received the mantle—a symbol of authority and power. He also received the double portion of Elijah's spirit, which he had boldly requested. This inheritance was not given lightly; it resulted from Elisha's unwavering loyalty and commitment.

Had Elisha left Elijah at any point, he would have missed the mantle. The anointing, the authority, and the double portion were all tied to his decision to stay connected, even when it seemed easier to walk away.

1. **Purpose Is Relational:** God often fulfills our purpose through relationships. Elisha's destiny was tied to Elijah, as

ours may be to mentors, leaders, or those who have gone before us in faith.

2. **Loyalty Builds Character:** The tests Elisha faced were not meant to discourage him but to reinforce his commitment. Loyalty is a vital part of preparation.

3. **Connection Requires Sacrifice:** Staying connected to Elijah meant Elisha had to leave behind his old life, endure the discomfort of the journey, and resist the temptation to quit.

4. **Promotion Comes Through Faithfulness:** Elisha's double portion was not given because of his ambition but because of his loyalty. God rewards those who honor the people and processes He places in their lives.

Lessons from Elisha's Journey

1. **Purpose Demands Pursuit:** We must actively pursue our purpose, even when faced with tests or opportunities to settle.

2. **Purpose Is Connected to People:** Elisha's destiny was tied to Elijah. Sometimes, God places us under the leadership or mentorship of others to prepare us for what lies ahead.

3. **Purpose Requires Endurance:** Every step of the journey—Gilgal, Bethel, Jericho, and the Jordan—was essential for Elisha to step into his calling. Skipping any part would have left him unprepared for the mantle.

Affirmation Prayer

Heavenly Father,

Thank You for the purpose You have placed within me. Even when the path seems complicated or unclear, please help me to remain steadfast and faithful. Like Elisha, give me the resolve to follow wherever You lead, knowing that my destiny is tied to my obedience. Strengthen my heart to persist through tests, endure through challenges, and trust in Your timing. I declare that I will not reject your purpose for my life. I will walk boldly, faithfully, and humbly, knowing that You have prepared the way. In Jesus' name, Amen.

Chapter 11
Frustrated Future

Key Verse: "Let us not grow weary in doing good, for at the proper time we will reap a harvest if we do not give up." (Galatians 6:9)

Frustration is an insidious tool of the enemy, designed to dismantle our focus, drain our strength, and weaken our resolve. It seeks to derail us, not by force but by persistence, whispering lies that what we are pursuing is too difficult, not worth the effort, or simply impossible. Frustration tests our will—it is a battlefield of perseverance where the stakes are high. If we allow frustration to consume us, we risk forfeiting our dreams and the divine destiny God has prepared for us.

Frustration is not merely an emotional response but a spiritual weapon the enemy uses to target our minds and wills. The Greek word for "weary" in Galatians 6:9 is ἐκκακέω (*ekkakeō*), meaning "to lose heart, to give up, or to become faint." This word encapsulates the enemy's ultimate goal: to make us lose heart and walk away from God's promises.

Frustration arises when the reality of our current circumstances collides with the hope of our future promises. It thrives in the gap between expectation and fulfillment, magnifying delays, obstacles, and disappointments. The enemy knows that most victories are won not by strength but by endurance, so he uses frustration to chip away at our resolve.

The story of Moses and the Israelites in the wilderness is a powerful example of how frustration tests our will and threatens our future. Delivered from Egypt by God's miraculous hand, the Israelites were on their way to the Promised Land. Yet, what should have been an 11-day journey turned into 40 years of wandering because frustration led them to doubt God's plan and rebel against His commands.

The Israelites repeatedly expressed their frustration, complaining about food, water, and the hardships of the desert. In Exodus 16:3, they said:

"If only we had died by the Lord's hand in Egypt! There we sat around pots of meat and ate all the food we wanted, but you have brought us out into this desert to starve this entire assembly to death."

This statement reveals the destructive power of frustration:

• **Distorted Memories:** Frustration caused the Israelites to idealize their slavery in Egypt, forgetting the oppression and suffering they endured.

• **Short-Sighted Focus:** Instead of focusing on the Promised Land ahead, they fixated on their immediate discomfort.

• **Rebellion Against Leadership:** Their frustration led them to grumble against Moses and, ultimately, against God Himself.

The Hebrew word for "grumble" is לָנוּן (*lanun*), which implies rebellion and complaint rooted in dissatisfaction.

Frustration blinded the Israelites to God's provision of manna, water, and protection, making them long for the very chains God had broken. You have to divorce your thoughts of the past.

Even Moses, a man of great faith, was not immune to frustration. In Numbers 20:7–12, God commanded Moses to speak to a rock to bring forth water for the people. Instead, Moses, overwhelmed by frustration with the Israelites' constant complaining, struck the rock twice with his staff. While water still flowed, Moses' disobedience cost him the opportunity to enter the Promised Land. Frustration will paralyze your now keeping from your future, and often, you won't get the chance again.

Frustration distorted Moses' judgment and caused him to act impulsively. His actions remind us that even great leaders can succumb to frustration if they do not guard their hearts and wills.

If not managed, frustration can cause us to forfeit the opportunities God places before us. It closes our eyes to His provision and paralyzes us with discouragement. Consider Elijah in 1 Kings 19:3-4, who, after a great victory on Mount Carmel, allowed frustration and fear to drive him into the wilderness, where he prayed to die. Elijah's emotions overwhelmed him, making him forget the power of God that had just been displayed. This moment reminds us that unchecked frustration can distort our view of reality and cause us to lose sight of God's faithfulness. Managing our emotions allows us to remain grounded in truth and prevents us from making decisions that undermine our calling.

Frustration also becomes a wall that hinders progress, tempting us to abandon our journey when the finish line is closer than we think. When we focus on our emotions instead of God's promises, we risk returning just before the breakthrough. Managing our emotions through prayer, reflection, and reliance on the Holy Spirit enables us to push through temporary setbacks and remain steadfast in our purpose. Frustration may come, but it does not have to define our response or hinder God's plans for our lives.

Frustration often intensifies just before a significant breakthrough or blessing. Why? Because the enemy recognizes the potential of what is coming and seeks to stop us before we reach it. Consider these truths:

1. **Frustration Reveals Our Weaknesses:** It exposes areas where our faith, patience, and trust in God must grow.

2. **Frustration Tests Our Commitment:** "Are you willing to persevere, even when it's hard? Will you trust God, even when the road is long?"

3. **Frustration Prepares Us for the Promise:** Just as a muscle grows stronger under resistance, frustration can refine our character and prepare us to handle God's blessings.

The Enemy is highly strategic with his frustration offers; it's a plow to self-destruct.

The enemy uses frustration to:

1. **Distort Perspective:** Frustration magnifies the problem and minimizes God's promises, making us feel trapped in our circumstances.

2. **Provoke Impatience:** It tempts us to take shortcuts or make rash decisions, leading to disobedience or failure.

3. **Weaken Resolve:** Prolonged frustration wears us down emotionally and spiritually, making quitting easier.

God planned an antidote for Overcoming the Test of Frustration.

1. **Anchor Yourself in God's Word:** Scripture is our weapon against frustration. Declare promises like Galatians 6:9, reminding yourself that perseverance will lead to a harvest.

2. **Pray Through Frustration:** Jesus modeled this in the Garden of Gethsemane. In His moment of anguish, He prayed, "Not my will, but Yours be done" (Luke 22:42). Prayer strengthens our will and aligns us with God's purposes.

3. **Keep Your Eyes on the Promise:** Focus on the future God has prepared for you, not the obstacles in front of you. Remember, frustration is temporary, but God's promises are eternal.

4. **Stay the Course:** Refuse to quit, no matter how hard it gets. The story of the Israelites reminds us that the Promised Land is worth the journey, even if the wilderness feels endless.

Frustration is not the end of the story. It is a test, a refining fire that shapes us for what lies ahead. Remember, the enemy uses frustration to make us quit, but God uses it to strengthen our resolve and prepare us for the promises He has already set in motion. Stand firm, and you will see the goodness of the Lord in the land of the living.

Affirmation Prayer

Heavenly Father,

Thank You for Your promises and the plans You have for my life. I acknowledge that frustration is a tool of the enemy, but I choose to stand firm in faith. Strengthen my will to persevere through delays, obstacles, and disappointments. When frustration clouds my vision, it reminds me of the harvest that awaits if I do not give up.

Help me to trust Your timing and provision, knowing that You are working all things together for my good. I declare that frustration will not cause me to quit, forfeit, or turn back. I will press forward, confident that the future You have prepared for me is more significant than any challenge I face.

In Jesus' name, Amen.

Chapter 12
The Power of the Anointing

Key Verses: "The Spirit of the Lord God is upon me; because the Lord has anointed me..." (Isaiah 61:1)

"And it shall come to pass in that day, that his burden shall be taken away from off thy shoulder, and his yoke from off thy neck, and the yoke shall be destroyed because of the anointing." (Isaiah 10:27)

"How God anointed Jesus of Nazareth with the Holy Spirit and power, and how he went around doing good and healing all who were under the power of the devil because God was with him." (Acts 10:38)

The anointing of God is not just a concept but a transformative reality that empowers believers to walk in divine purpose and authority. From the intricate preparation of the anointing oil in the Old Testament to the life and ministry of Jesus Christ, the anointing represents God's supernatural presence and power at work in and through His people. It is the driving force behind liberation, healing, and the destruction of all forms of bondage.

The anointing is a sacred empowerment God gives us to fulfill His divine purposes. It is not something we can earn or manufacture; it is a supernatural impartation from the Holy Spirit. The anointing is what transforms ordinary individuals into vessels of extraordinary impact. Whether in ministry, leadership, or everyday life, the anointing equips us to operate in God's strength rather than our own.

It is not just for preaching or performing miracles but for breaking yokes of bondage, bringing healing to the brokenhearted, and advancing God's kingdom in every sphere of influence. You can do no function for God that doesn't require an anointing.

The Anointing in the Old Testament

The anointing oil in the Old Testament physically represented a spiritual reality. In Exodus 30:22–33, God instructed Moses to create a sacred anointing oil, giving precise details about its ingredients and use. Each oil element carried symbolic meaning, pointing to the holiness and purpose of the anointing.

The Ingredients of the Anointing Oil

1. Pure Myrrh (12½ pounds) 500 shekel

Myrrh is a resin that comes from the bark of the myrrh tree. Its extraction requires the tree to be pierced, symbolizing suffering and sacrifice. Myrrh represents purification, humility, and the sweet fragrance of obedience to God.

2. Sweet Cinnamon (6¼ pounds) 250 shekel

Cinnamon is harvested from the bark of a tree and is known for its warmth and fragrance. It symbolizes the zeal, passion, and fire of the Holy Spirit. The sweetness reminds us that the anointing should bring joy and life to those it touches.

3. Sweet Cane or Calamus (6¼ pounds) 250 shekel

Calamus is a reed plant that grows in swampy areas, symbolizing upright connection and the ability to thrive under challenging conditions. It speaks of integrity and the grace to stand firm amid challenges.

4. Cassia (12½ pounds) 500 shekel

Cassia is a spice from the cinnamon family, often used in cleansing rituals. It represents sanctification, submission, dreams, and a vision of God's authority. It must weigh the same as your sacrifice and suffering.

5. Olive Oil (as the base)

Olive oil, the base of the anointing oil, comes from crushed olives, symbolizing the process of consecration and the outpouring of the Holy Spirit.

Each ingredient was carefully measured and blended, emphasizing the precision and intentionality of the anointing. This oil was used to consecrate priests, kings, and sacred objects, setting them apart for divine purposes. The Hebrew word for "anoint" is מָשַׁח (*mashach*), meaning "to smear, consecrate, or set apart."

Jesus was the prime example of the anointing.

Acts 10:38 declares, *"How God anointed Jesus of Nazareth with the Holy Spirit and power, and how he went about doing good and healing all who were under the power of the devil because God was with him."*

This verse provides a powerful summary of Jesus' earthly ministry and highlights three key aspects of the anointing:

1. **Anointed with the Holy Spirit and Power:** The Greek word for "anointed" is (*chriō*), which means "to consecrate or set apart for a special task." God anointed Jesus with the Holy Spirit (, *Pneuma Hagion*) and power (*dynamis*), equipping Him to operate in divine authority.

2. **Doing Good:** The anointing empowered Jesus to serve others selflessly. Healing, teaching, and performing miracles were all expressions of His anointing.

3. **Destroying the Works of the Devil:** Jesus' anointing was not just for physical healing but also spiritual liberation, breaking the power of sin, sickness, and oppression.

The anointing on Jesus was not passive—it was active, purposeful, and transformative. Every act of kindness, healing, and deliverance flowed from the anointing that rested upon Him. A lack of kindness could be a sign you lack the anointing.

The Anointing: A Yoke-Destroying Power

Isaiah 10:27 declares, *"The yoke shall be destroyed because of the anointing."* The Hebrew word for "destroyed" is עוֹל (*chabal*), meaning "to break, ruin, or render useless." The anointing doesn't merely loosen the yoke; it destroys it, ensuring it can never be enslaved again.

The "yoke" symbolizes bondage, whether spiritual, emotional, or physical. Through the anointing, Jesus came to destroy the enemy's works (1 John 3:8). His mission was to heal or comfort and eradicate the root causes of oppression, restoring freedom and wholeness to humanity.

Jesus and Isaiah 61: The Fulfillment of the Anointing

In Luke 4:18–19, Jesus reads from Isaiah 61 in the synagogue, declaring:

"The Spirit of the Lord is upon Me because He has anointed Me to preach the gospel to the poor; He has sent Me to heal the brokenhearted, to proclaim liberty to the captives and recovery of sight to the blind, to set at liberty those who are oppressed; to proclaim the acceptable year of the Lord."

Here, Jesus identifies Himself as the fulfillment of Isaiah's prophecy. The anointing on His life was not abstract; it was specific and mission-driven, empowering Him to:

• **Preach Good News:** To the poor, marginalized, and hopeless.

• **Heal the Brokenhearted:** Bringing emotional and spiritual restoration.

• **Proclaim Liberty:** Breaking the chains of sin and captivity.

• **Give Sight to the Blind:** Both physically and spiritually.

• **Set the Oppressed Free:** Breaking demonic strongholds and bringing peace.

The anointing fueled every facet of Jesus' ministry. He modeled what it means to walk in the Spirit, demonstrating that the anointing is given not for personal gain but for the benefit of others and the advancement of God's kingdom. It can be an occasional anointing, it must rest on you, or it's just a show.

The Anointing and Spiritual Warfare

Jesus' anointing also positioned Him as a spiritual warrior. Acts 10:38 emphasizes that He healed *"all who were under the power of the devil."* The Greek word for "oppressed" **καταδυναστευόμενος**, (*katadynasteuomenos*) means "to be held down by tyranny." The anointing broke through demonic oppression, establishing Jesus as the ultimate liberator.

This same anointing is available to believers through the Holy Spirit (1 John 2:20, 27). Walking in the anointing, we are called to confront and dismantle the enemy's schemes, bringing healing, freedom, and restoration wherever we go.

Protecting the Anointing

Ecclesiastes 10:1 warns, *"Dead flies putrefy the perfumer's ointment and cause it to give off a foul odor."* The anointing is precious and must be protected from contamination. Just as flies can spoil ointment, sin, compromise, distractions, and destructive behaviors can diminish the effectiveness of the anointing in our lives.

Here are some Ways to Protect the Anointing

1. **Pursue Holiness:** Live a life consecrated to God, avoiding sin and temptation.

2. **Stay Aligned with the Spirit:** Regular prayer and communion with God keep the anointing fresh and active.

3. **Guard Your Heart:** Protect against bitterness, pride, and complacency.

4. **Remain Humble:** The anointing is not about us but God's glory.

5. **Guard Your Environment:** Surround yourself with people and influences that honor the anointing on your life.

Our Anointing Today

The anointing that rested on Jesus is now available to us through the Holy Spirit. Isaiah 61 and Acts 10:38 are not just historical records but blueprints for our lives. We are called to:

• Preach the good news.

• Heal the brokenhearted.

• Set captives free.

• Break the yoke of oppression.

The anointing empowers us to walk in the authority of Christ, bringing His kingdom to earth. The anointing is a sacred trust. It equips us to do the works of Jesus, advancing His kingdom and destroying the enemy's works.

The anointing also requires stewardship and reverence. Just as the Old Testament anointing oil was made with precise ingredients and used exclusively for consecrated purposes (Exodus 30:22–33), the anointing on our lives must be honored and respected. It is not for self-promotion or personal gain but to serve others and glorify God. Misusing or allowing the anointing to be contaminated through sin, pride, or neglect can diminish its effectiveness.

Finally, the anointing carries excellent power but with great power comes great responsibility. It is not given for our benefit alone but for the liberation and blessing of others. This mandate requires us to go beyond ourselves, stepping into places of darkness and brokenness to bring God's light and hope. The anointing is not a static gift but a dynamic force that grows as we obey God's call. When we steward the anointing well, it becomes a powerful instrument through which God works to transform lives and bring His kingdom to earth.

Affirmation Prayer

Heavenly Father,

Thank You for the anointing of the Holy Spirit that empowers me to walk in Your purpose. Just as You anointed Jesus to preach, heal, and deliver, I ask for the same anointing to rest upon my life. Let Your Spirit flow through me, destroying every yoke and bringing freedom to those in bondage.

Teach me to protect the anointing by living a life of holiness and humility. Help me to stay aligned with Your will, always seeking Your glory over my own. I declare that I will walk in the power of the anointing, fulfilling the purpose You have set before me.

In Jesus' name, Amen.

Chapter 13
Called to Serve

"For even the Son of Man did not come to be served, but to serve, and to give His life as a ransom for many." (Mark 10:45)

The essence of every divine calling is service. At its core, being called by God is not about status, recognition, or personal gain but about pouring out our lives in service to others. Our calling is stewardship, a sacred trust to carry out God's work by serving His people. Mismanaging that service—whether through neglect, manipulation, or selfish ambition—undermines the very purpose of the call. Being a servant is the highest calling in the kingdom of God. Jesus taught that greatness is measured not by power or position but by humility and a willingness to serve others. In Matthew 23:11, He declared, *"The greatest among you will be your servant."* This statement turns the world's values upside down, reminding us that servanthood is the true path to significance. A servant's heart prioritizes the needs of others over personal ambition, reflecting the selfless love of Christ. In serving, we become most like Him, fulfilling His command to love one another as He has loved us (John 13:34).

A servant must embrace the humility that comes with their role. Humility is not thinking less of oneself but thinking of oneself less. True servanthood requires us to set aside pride, entitlement, and the desire for recognition. Philippians 2:3–4 instructs us, *"Do nothing out of selfish ambition or vain conceit. Rather, in humility value others above yourselves, not looking to your interests but each of you to the interests of others."* This mindset is essential for serving well, ensuring our motives remain pure and focused on glorifying God rather than seeking personal gain. A humble servant will go unnoticed, trusting that God sees their work and will reward them in His time. And whatsoever ye do, do it heartily, as to the Lord, and not unto men;[24] Knowing that of the Lord ye shall receive the reward of the inheritance: for ye serve the Lord Christ.

"And whatsoever ye do, do it heartily, as to the Lord, and not unto men; Knowing that of the Lord ye shall receive the reward of the inheritance: for ye serve the Lord Christ." Colossians 3:23-24

Being a servant also means being faithful to the small things. Jesus taught in Luke 16:10, *"Whoever is faithful in very little is also faithful in much."* Sometimes serving may seem mundane or insignificant, but these moments are opportunities to demonstrate our commitment and obedience to God. Whether cleaning a space, encouraging someone, or simply listening, every service carries eternal value when done for the Lord. Servants must remember that they are custodians of their gifts, time, and resources, not owners. By serving faithfully, we honor God and create an atmosphere where His love and grace can flow freely through us to impact others.

Being called to serve means extending love, compassion, and help to all people, regardless of their background, status, or ability to repay. The parable of the Good

Samaritan in Luke 10:25–37 illustrates this beautifully. When a man was beaten and left for dead, it was not the priest or the Levite—those expected to help—who stopped, but a Samaritan, someone from a group despised by the Jews. The Samaritan crossed cultural and social barriers to serve someone in desperate need, asking nothing in return. His actions demonstrate that proper service is not about what we can gain but about meeting the needs of others with selfless love. This story challenges us to evaluate whether we are willing to serve those different from us, those who may never be able to repay our kindness, and even those society deems unworthy.

God's call to serve extends beyond our comfort zones or personal preferences. It is easy to serve those who can benefit us or whom we find relatable. Still, true servanthood mirrors the heart of God, who shows no favoritism (Acts 10:34). Jesus' ministry modeled this inclusivity as He served tax collectors, sinners, the marginalized, and even His enemies. When we limit our service to those who align with our expectations or who might reciprocate, we distort the essence of our calling. Serving all people, as the Good Samaritan did, reflects Christ's unconditional love and brings His kingdom closer to earth. It reminds us that every person, regardless of their circumstances, is created in God's image and worthy of dignity, compassion, and care. True servanthood calls us to look beyond social barriers, prejudices, or personal gain and extend our hands to anyone in need, embodying the love and grace of God.

Service is the heart of our calling service, which is not just an act but an attitude, a way of life that reflects God's heart. When God calls us, we are called to serve others as His hands and feet in the world. The Greek word for "serve" διακονέω (*diakoneó*) means "to minister, to attend to the needs of others." It emphasizes action driven by humility and love.

Why Are We Called to Serve?

1. **To Reflect God's Character:** God is a servant at heart. Scripture shows Him caring for His people, providing for their needs, and guiding them with love. When we serve, we reflect His nature.

2. **To Build God's Kingdom:** Service is how we carry out God's mission on earth—bringing hope to the hopeless, healing to the broken, and justice to the oppressed.

3. **To Fulfill the Law of Love:** Galatians 5:13 says, *"Through love serve one another."* Love is the foundation of service. It compels us to prioritize others above ourselves.

Jesus, The Ultimate Servant

The most excellent example of servanthood is found in Jesus Christ. Though He was the Son of God, He humbled Himself to serve humanity. Philippians 2:5–7 declares:

"Let this mind be in you which was also in Christ Jesus, who, being in the form of God, did not consider it robbery to be equal with God, but made Himself of no reputation,

taking the form of a bondservant, and coming in the likeness of men."

1. Jesus Served Selflessly:

In John 13:3–5, Jesus washed His disciples' feet—a task typically reserved for servants. He did this knowing He was the Son of God, illustrating that no act of service is beneath us.

2. Jesus Served Sacrificially:

Mark 10:45 reminds us that Jesus came not to be served but to serve, ultimately giving His life as a ransom for many. His sacrifice was the ultimate act of service, showing us that accurate service requires selflessness and a willingness to lay down our lives for others.

3. Jesus Served with Compassion:

Throughout His ministry, Jesus was moved with compassion for the multitudes, healing the sick, feeding the hungry, and teaching the lost. His service was driven by love, not obligation.

The Dangers of Mismanaging Service

When called to serve, we must approach our calling with humility, integrity, and a pure heart. Mismanaging service can cause harm to the people we are called to serve and dishonor God. Below are some ways we can fall into the trap of mismanaging service:

1. Manipulating Those We Serve

Serving others is not an opportunity to control, manipulate, or exploit them. Whether through guilt, coercion, or selfish ambition, using people for personal gain violates the trust that comes with our calling. Ezekiel 34:2–4 warns against leaders who misuse their positions:

"Woe to the shepherds of Israel who feed themselves! Should not the shepherds feed the flocks? You eat the fat and clothe yourselves with the wool; you slaughter the fatlings but do not feed the flock."

True servanthood seeks the good of others, not personal benefit. Manipulation undermines the very heart of service.

2. Neglecting Those We Are Called to Serve

We fail in our assignment when we ignore or neglect the needs of those we are called to serve. Matthew 25:45 warns, *"Whatever you did not do for one of the least of these, you did not do for Me."* Service requires attentiveness and compassion. Neglect can stem from pride, distraction, or a lack of love but ultimately dishonors God.

3. Serving for Recognition or Reward

Jesus cautioned against serving with selfish motives in Matthew 6:1:

"Take heed that you do not do your charitable deeds before men, to be seen by them. Otherwise, you have no reward from your Father in heaven."

Service rooted in pride seeks applause and approval from others rather than the glory of God. Genuine service is content to go unnoticed, knowing that God sees all.

Servanthood will Require real Sacrifice, not just lip service

Service can be challenging and inconvenient. It requires humility, patience, and a willingness to put others' needs above ours. Romans 12:1 reminds us to offer our lives as *"a living sacrifice, holy and acceptable to God, which is your reasonable service."* This means:

1. **Serving Even When It Costs Us:**

True service requires time, energy, and resources. We must be willing to give of ourselves without expecting anything in return.

2. **Serving Even When It's Inconvenient:**

Jesus served the multitudes even when He was tired, hungry, or grieving. In Matthew 14:13–14, after hearing of John the Baptist's death, Jesus sought solitude but was met by a large crowd. Moved with compassion, He healed their sick and fed over 5,000 people.

3. **Serving Even Those Who Hurt Us:**

Jesus washed the feet of Judas, knowing he would betray Him. This profound humility reminds us that service is not conditional on others' behavior but a reflection of God's unconditional love.

How to Serve Well

1. Serve with Humility:

Philippians 2:3 says, *"Do nothing out of selfish ambition or vain conceit. Rather, in humility, value others above yourselves."* Genuine service begins with a posture of humility.

2. Serve with Integrity:

Colossians 3:23 reminds us, *"Whatever you do, work at it with all your heart, as working for the Lord, not for human masters."* Serve with excellence and honesty, knowing that God is your ultimate audience.

3. Serve with Love:

1 Corinthians 13:3 warns that even great acts of service are meaningless without love. Let love be the driving force behind all you do.

4. Serve Reliant on God:

Service can be exhausting, but we can endure when we rely on God's strength through prayer. Isaiah 40:31 promises, *"Those who wait on the Lord shall renew their strength."*

Serving others is both a privilege and a responsibility. It is the purpose of our calling and the heart of God's kingdom.

Let us serve well, with integrity and love, always remembering that we serve not just people but the Lord Himself.

Affirmation Prayer

Heavenly Father,

Thank You for calling me to serve. Help me to approach my calling with humility, love, and integrity. Guard my heart against pride, manipulation, or neglect. Teach me to value others above myself and to serve with the same selflessness and compassion that Jesus modeled.

I surrender my time, energy, and resources to You, knowing that genuine service requires sacrifice. Strengthen me to serve even when difficult, inconvenient, or unnoticed. May my service bring glory to Your name and reflect Your love to the world.

In Jesus' name, Amen.

Chapter 14
Called to Pray

"Pray without ceasing." (1 Thessalonians 5:17)

Every calling from God no matter the assignment, demands a life of prayer. Prayer is not merely a spiritual discipline, but the lifeline for those God has called. In prayer, we hear God's voice, receive His guidance, and find the strength to carry out His will. Throughout Scripture, we see that those who were used mightily by God were also people of fervent prayer. Most importantly, Jesus Himself, modeled a life deeply rooted in prayer.

Prayer Is The Foundation of Every Calling

When God calls us, He calls us to Himself first. Ministry, leadership, or any service is secondary to our relationship with Him. Prayer is the primary means through which that relationship is nurtured. It is in the secret place of prayer that:

We Receive Instructions: Prayer connects us to God's heart and purposes. Jeremiah 33:3 says, *"Call to Me, and I will answer you and show you great and mighty things, which you do not know."* Through prayer, we clarify our calling and direction for our journey.

We Are Empowered: Prayer is where we draw spiritual strength. Isaiah 40:31 declares, *"But those who wait on the Lord shall renew their strength; they shall mount up with wings like eagles, they shall run and not be weary, they* *shall walk and not faint."* Every calling comes with challenges, but we are fortified to persevere through prayer.

We Align with God's Will: Jesus taught us to pray, *"Your kingdom come, Your will be done on earth as it is in heaven" (Matthew 6:10). Prayer aligns our hearts with God's will, ensuring that we are not operating in our strength or pursuing our agendas.

The Prayer Life of Jesus

No one exemplifies the necessity of prayer better than Jesus. Though He was entirely God, He lived as fully man, dependent on prayer to sustain His ministry. The Gospels frequently mention Jesus withdrawing to pray, often during pivotal moments of His life and ministry.

Prayer in Solitude:

"But Jesus often withdrew to lonely places and prayed." (Luke 5:16)

Jesus prioritized solitary prayer, seeking the Father's presence away from the distractions of the crowd. His example reminds us that public ministry is fueled by private devotion.

Prayer Before Major Decisions:

Before selecting the twelve apostles, Jesus spent the entire night in prayer:

"Now it came to pass in those days that He went out to the mountain to pray and continued all night in prayer to God. And when it was day, He called His disciples to Himself;

and from them, He chose twelve whom He also named apostles." (Luke 6:12–13)

This teaches us that prayer is essential for discerning God's will, especially when making significant decisions.

Prayer in Times of Pressure:

In the Garden of Gethsemane, as He faced the cross, Jesus prayed fervently:

"Father, if it is Your will, take this cup away from Me; nevertheless, not My will, but Yours, be done." (Luke 22:42)

Prayer was where Jesus surrendered His will to the Father, finding strength to fulfill His mission. His agony in prayer shows us that even in the most challenging moments, prayer can sustain and empower us.

Prayer for Others:

Jesus also interceded for His disciples and future believers:

"I pray for them. I do not pray for the world but for those whom You have given Me, for they are Yours." (John 17:9)

This high priestly prayer demonstrates the importance of interceding for others as part of our calling.

The Significance of Prayer in Our Calling

Prayer Keeps Us Dependent on God:

The essence of prayer is humility—recognizing that we cannot fulfill our calling in strength. Jesus said, *"Apart from Me you can do nothing" (John 15:5). Through prayer, we stay connected to the source of our strength and wisdom.

2. **Prayer Builds Spiritual Sensitivity:**

In prayer, we attune our hearts to the voice of the Holy Spirit, who leads and guides us. Romans 8:26 reminds us, *"The Spirit also helps in our weaknesses. For we do not know what we should pray for as we ought, but the Spirit Himself makes intercession for us with groanings which cannot be uttered."*

3. **Prayer Guards Against Burnout:**

Ministry and calling can be exhausting, but prayer provides spiritual renewal. Jesus, though often surrounded by crowds, took time to pray and recharge. His rhythm of work and rest in prayer is a model for us to follow.

4. **Prayer Is a Weapon in Spiritual Warfare:**

Every calling will face opposition, but prayer is our defense. Ephesians 6:18 commands us to pray *"always with all prayer and supplication in the Spirit, being watchful to this end with all perseverance."* Through prayer, we overcome the schemes of the enemy.

Called to Pray Without Ceasing

Paul's exhortation to "pray without ceasing" (1 Thessalonians 5:17) reminds us that prayer is not confined to specific times or places. A continual posture of the heart—a constant communion with God- fuels every aspect of our calling.

- **In the Morning:** Start the day in prayer, seeking God's guidance and strength.

- **Throughout the Day:** Whisper prayers in moments of decision, difficulty, or gratitude.

- **In the Evening:** Reflect on the day and surrender any burdens to God.

Prayer is not about ritual but relationship. The ongoing conversation keeps us rooted in God's presence and purpose.

A Life of Prayer will always accompany a Life of Purpose Elijah, the prophet, is a person whose life was marked by prayer. Bold prophetic declarations and miraculous interventions characterized his ministry, yet his intimate relationship with God through prayer empowered him. James 5:17–18 highlights Elijah's prayer life, stating that *"Elijah was a man with a nature like ours, and he prayed earnestly that it would not rain; and it did not rain on the land for three years and six months. And he prayed again, and the heaven gave rain, and the earth produced its fruit."* Elijah's effectiveness in ministry was not due to personal strength or eloquence but his commitment to seeking God in prayer. His prayers were fervent, persistent, and lined up with God's will, showing that prayer was not just an act for Elijah but the essence of his calling.

The term "callused knees" has been used metaphorically to describe those, like Elijah, who spend so much time praying on their knees that it becomes evident in their lives. Elijah's "callused knees" symbolize his reliance on God for direction, provision, and intervention. In 1 Kings 18:42, after confronting the prophets of Baal, Elijah went up to Mount Carmel, bowed to the ground, and placed his face between his knees to pray for rain. This posture reflected his deep humility and dependence on God. Despite the delay in seeing results—his servant reported no sign of rain six times—Elijah persisted in prayer until the seventh report confirmed a small cloud forming. This moment underscores that Elijah's faith in God's promise was sustained through his dedication to prayer, even when the evidence of change seemed nonexistent.

Elijah's life reminds us that prayer is about asking for miracles and cultivating a deep, unshakable connection with God. His ability to stand boldly before kings and call down fire from heaven came from his private moments of kneeling before God. The power to confront, overcome, and lead was birthed in the secret place of prayer. Like Elijah, we are called to develop "callused knees," symbolizing a life marked by continual, sincere, and humble prayer. In these moments, we draw strength, receive guidance, and parallel ourselves with God's will, enabling us to fulfill the unique call He has placed on our lives. Elijah's prayer life challenges us to prioritize our time with God and trust in His timing and promises, no matter how long the wait may seem.

If God has called you, He has also called you to pray. Just as Jesus depended on prayer to fulfill His mission, we must do the same. The magnitude of our calling is directly tied to the depth of our prayer life. Without prayer, we risk operating in our strength, which will eventually fail. But with prayer, we remain connected to God, empowered by His Spirit, and aligned with His will. Prayer is not optional for those who are called; it is essential. Let us embrace the life of prayer, knowing that it is our lifeline to the God who has called us and the source of every good thing we need to accomplish His will.

Affirmation Prayer

Heavenly Father,

Thank You for the calling You have placed on my life. I acknowledge that I cannot fulfill it without You. Teach me to have a prayer life, seeking Your face in every season and circumstance. Just as Jesus often withdrew to pray, help me to prioritize time with You, knowing that it is the source of my strength, wisdom, and direction.

Guard my heart from distraction and keep me sensitive to the leading of Your Spirit. May my prayer life be vibrant and consistent, empowering me to walk boldly in my calling. I declare that I am called to pray, and through prayer, I will fulfill the purpose You have set before me.

In Jesus' name, Amen.

Chapter 15
Surviving Assassination Attempts

Key Verse: "No weapon formed against you shall prosper, and every tongue which rises against you in judgment You shall condemn. This is the heritage of the servants of the Lord, and their righteousness is from Me," says the Lord." (Isaiah 54:17)

Life is filled with challenges, opposition, and even outright attacks on your character, purpose, or mission. While most will never face a literal assassination attempt, we all encounter spiritual, emotional, or relational attempts to derail us. These "assassination attempts" are often designed to distract, dishearten, or destroy our focus. But with God as our protector, no weapon formed against us will prosper, though weapons may indeed be formed. Surviving these moments requires discernment, trust in God, and the wisdom to know when silence is the most powerful response.

On March 30, 1981, John Hinckley Jr. attempted to assassinate President Ronald Reagan outside the Washington Hilton Hotel. As Reagan exited the building, Hinckley fired six shots in 1.7 seconds, hitting Reagan and three others. Reagan, though critically wounded, survived the attempt. Why did the assassination fail? Many factors contributed, including quick action by the Secret Service and Reagan's physical resilience. However, Reagan's survival also underscored a more profound principle:

attacks, no matter how well-planned, do not have to succeed.

The Reagan assassination attempt teaches us that survival is often a combination of preparation, resilience, and divine providence. His ability to recover and continue leading the nation is a metaphor for how we, too, can recover from attacks on our mission or character. What is crucial to note is that Reagan did not retaliate with anger or fear but moved forward with grace and confidence. This approach mirrors biblical wisdom that not every attack requires a response. Proverbs 26:4 says, *"Do not answer a fool according to his folly, or you will be just like him."*

When we face "assassination attempts" in life—be they in the form of slander, betrayal, or outright opposition—it is tempting to respond immediately, defending ourselves or retaliating. However, not every attack warrants our energy. Jesus Himself modeled this in His response to His accusers. During His trial, when falsely accused, Jesus remained silent, fulfilling the prophecy in Isaiah 53:7: *"He was oppressed and afflicted, yet He did not open His mouth."* His silence was not weakness but strength, demonstrating His trust in the Father's ultimate justice.

Similarly, when pursued by Saul, David chose not to retaliate even though he had multiple opportunities to do so. In 1 Samuel 24:10, David said to Saul, *"I will not stretch out my hand against my lord, for he is the Lord's anointed."* David understood that God fights our battles and that responding to every attack can distract us from our greater purpose. Surviving assassination attempts—

whether literal or metaphorical—requires the wisdom to discern which battles are worth engaging in and which are best left to God.

The Power of Resilience and Trust

Surviving an assassination attempt, whether physical or spiritual, requires resilience. Resilience is the capacity to recover quickly from difficulties. It is not just physical strength but emotional and spiritual fortitude. Ronald Reagan's survival was not just about escaping bullets; it was about his ability to continue his mission despite the trauma. Likewise, as believers, our resilience is rooted in our faith in God's protection and promises.

Isaiah 54:17 assures us that *"no weapon formed against you shall prosper."* This scripture does not mean weapons will not be formed; it means they will not achieve their intended purpose. Attacks may come, but with God as our shield, they cannot derail His plan for our lives. Surviving such attacks requires trust in His sovereignty and a refusal to be consumed by fear or retaliation. Resilience allows us to recover, refocus, and rise stronger from adversity.

Responding with Purpose, Not Emotion

1. **Discern When to Speak:** Not every attack requires a public defense. When paired with prayer and trust in God, silence can be a robust response.

2. **Stay Focused on Your Mission:** Assassination attempts are often designed to distract you. Refrain from losing sight of your calling, even in the face of opposition.

3. **Rely on God's Justice:** Romans 12:19 reminds us, *"Do not take revenge, my dear friends, but leave room for God's wrath, for it is written: 'It is mine to avenge; I will repay,' says the Lord."* Trust God to vindicate you in His time.

Lessons from Assassination Attempts

1. **Preparation Matters:** Just as Reagan's Secret Service team was trained to respond quickly, we must prepare spiritually through prayer, studying God's Word, and building a strong foundation of faith.

2. **Resilience Is Key:** Like Reagan's recovery and return to leadership, we must bounce back from life's attacks with determination and grace.

3. **God Is Our Shield:** Ultimately, God preserves us. Psalm 91:4 declares, *"He will cover you with His feathers, and under His wings, you will find refuge; His faithfulness will be your shield and rampart."*

Assassination attempts—emotional or spiritual—are part of life's challenges, but they do not have to define us. With God's protection, wisdom, and resilience, we can survive and thrive, fulfilling the purpose for which we were created.

Affirmation Prayer

Heavenly Father,

Thank You for being my protector and shield against every attack. Teach me to trust You when I face opposition, knowing that no weapon formed against me will prosper.

Help me discern when to speak and remain silent, relying on Your justice and timing.

Strengthen my heart to remain resilient despite adversity, focused on the mission You have given me. I declare that every plan of the enemy will fail, and Your purpose for my life will prevail. Guide me to respond with grace, wisdom, and courage, reflecting Your love in all I do.

In Jesus' name, Amen.

Chapter 16
Becoming a Living Epistle

Key Verse: "You are our epistle written in our hearts, known and read by all men." (2 Corinthians 3:2)

As believers, our lives are not just about the words we speak or our prayers—they are the stories we live. Paul describes Christians as "living epistles," letters written not with ink but by the Spirit of God, known and read by everyone we encounter. This profound truth reminds us that our lives are a testimony, a reflection of Christ's work within us. Every action, decision, and response contribute's to the narrative others see and experience. We are the gospel in motion, embodying God's grace, truth, and love for a watching world.

The Message of a Living Epistle

An epistle is a letter, a written communication meant to convey a message. When Paul calls believers "epistles," he highlights that our lives communicate a divine message to the world. The content of this "letter" is the gospel's transformative power. Our lives reveal how Christ has redeemed us, His Spirit sanctifies us, and His love compels us to serve others.

However, unlike a traditional letter, a living epistle is ongoing. Every day adds new paragraphs, chapters, and verses to the story God writes in and through us. Philippians 1:27 urges us to *"conduct yourselves in a manner worthy of the gospel of Christ"* because our lives may be the only Bible some people will ever read. This responsibility calls us to integrity, humility, and constant pursuit of Christlikeness.

Paul continues in 2 Corinthians 3:3, *"You are a letter from Christ… written not with ink but with the Spirit of the living God, not on tablets of stone but on tablets of human hearts."* This verse underscores that our transformation is not self-manufactured; it is the work of the Holy Spirit. The Greek word for "written" ἐγγράφω (*engrapho*) means to engrave or inscribe deeply, signifying that God's truth is permanently etched into our lives.

Our character, decisions, and relationships are shaped by the Spirit, who continually writes Christ's story into our hearts. This divine authorship ensures that our message is authentic, rooted not in human effort but in God's power. As living epistles, we are called to cooperate with the Spirit, allowing Him to mold us into vessels that reflect His glory.

Being Read by All Men

Living as an epistle means understanding that people are always watching. Friends, family, coworkers, and even strangers observe how we navigate life—our trials, victories, and daily interactions. What they "read" in us often shapes their understanding of who God is. This is both a privilege and a responsibility.

Jesus highlighted this principle in Matthew 5:14–16, saying, *"You are the light of the world... let your light shine before others, that they may see your good deeds and glorify your Father in heaven."* Our lives should point people to Christ, offering hope, encouragement, and a glimpse of His love. However, this requires intentionality. Just as an author carefully chooses words to convey a message, we must live purposefully, ensuring that our actions align with the truth we profess.

To become a living epistle is to embrace the idea that our lives are not our own. We are part of a greater narrative—God's redemptive story for humanity. This requires us to live transparently, acknowledging our weaknesses and celebrating God's grace. It also means consistently striving to reflect Christ in every area of our lives.

Like any story, a living epistle has both challenges and triumphs. There will be moments when our faith is tested, our actions fall short, or our message is misunderstood. Yet, even in these moments, God's grace shines through, reminding us and others that His power is made perfect in weakness (2 Corinthians 12:9). Our willingness to trust Him through every chapter of our lives becomes a powerful testimony to His faithfulness.

How to Be a Living Epistle

1. **Live Authentically:** Allow Christ to work through your imperfections. Be genuine in your faith, showing others how God's grace transforms and sustains you.

2. **Walk in Integrity:** Let your actions align with your beliefs. Colossians 3:17 says, *"Whatever you do, whether in word or deed, do it all in the name of the Lord Jesus."*

3. **Stay Connected to the Author:** Daily prayer, study of the Word, and sensitivity to the Holy Spirit ensure that God remains the writer of your story.

4. **Reflect Christ's Love:** Show kindness, compassion, and forgiveness in every interaction. Let people see Christ in how you treat them.

5. **Encourage Others:** Use your life as a platform to uplift and inspire others in their journeys. Share your testimony boldly and honestly.

Being a living epistle is a lifelong journey. As God continues to write His story through us, we are privileged to be His message of hope and redemption to the world. Let us live intentionally, allowing our lives to point others to the Author of salvation.

Affirmation Prayer

Heavenly Father,

Thank You for making my life a living epistle, written by Your Spirit and read by those around me. Help me to live authentically and boldly, reflecting Your love, grace, and truth in all I do. Teach me to walk in integrity, allowing my actions to align with the gospel's message.

Write your story on my heart daily, and use my life to draw others closer to You. May I be a light in the darkness and a testimony of Your transformative power. I surrender every chapter of my life to You, trusting that You, the Author and Finisher of my faith, will complete the good work You have begun.

In Jesus' name, Amen.

Chapter 17
Life on Stage

Key Verse: "All things are lawful for me, but not all things are helpful; all things are lawful for me, but not all things edify." (1 Corinthians 10:23)

Life on stage is a reality for anyone called to a position of influence or leadership. Whether you're a public figure, spiritual leader, athlete, or professional, your actions, words, and associations carry weight. In a world where social media amplifies every move, your life becomes a story for others to observe and interpret. Platforms and decisions, once private, now have public implications. As believers, our lives are not just about ourselves but reflections of Christ. This requires us to live with wisdom and intentionality, guarding both our reputation and the integrity of our calling.

The Double-Edged Sword of Social Media

Social media is one of the most powerful tools of modern influence. It allows instant connection, offering a platform to share encouragement, spread the gospel, or build relationships. However, it also has the potential to undermine your influence. What you post, comment, or endorse shapes the perception of who you are and what you stand for. Proverbs 18:21 reminds us, *"Death and life are in the power of the tongue,"* in the digital age, this extends to every word, photo, or video shared online.

Reckless use of social media can damage credibility, even if unintentional. Posts that appear divisive, offensive, or contrary to your values can harm your mission and cause others to stumble. Romans 14:16 reminds us, *"Let not your good be evil spoken of."* Even well-meaning actions can be misunderstood if not presented with care. This principle calls for discernment in how we engage online, ensuring that what we intend for good is not a source of confusion or harm.

Our digital footprint should align with the values of our faith, reflecting Christ's love and truth. This requires intentionality and restraint, knowing that the online stage magnifies every word and action. A single post can build bridges or burn them, so we must steward this platform with humility and wisdom.

Guarding Your Associations

When you enter a position of influence, your company reflects your character and values. Specific roles require stricter boundaries in relationships to maintain credibility and integrity. For instance, NCAA athletes sign agreements that limit their activities and associations. A particular rule restricts them from participating in playground or recreational basketball games once signed, even though these games are not inherently wrong. This boundary exists to protect their eligibility, avoid unnecessary injuries, and preserve the integrity of their position as collegiate athletes.

Similarly, law enforcement officers are prohibited from fraternizing with convicted felons, gang members, or drug dealers, as such relationships can compromise their role and the public's trust. In the same way, as believers and leaders, we must exercise discernment in our associations. While we are called to love and reach all people, we must guard against connections that could jeopardize our witness or misrepresent our faith. 2 Corinthians 6:14 reminds us, *"Do not be unequally yoked with unbelievers. For what partnership has righteousness with lawlessness?"*

This principle is not about isolation but about wisdom. The people you associate with can either enhance your influence or damage your credibility. Living on stage means being intentional about your relationships and understanding that some connections, though lawful, may not be beneficial to your calling.

Everything Lawful Isn't Expedient

The apostle Paul's statement in 1 Corinthians 10:23, *"All things are lawful, but not all things are helpful,"* underscores the importance of discernment. Just because something is permissible doesn't mean it is beneficial. As a leader or influencer, your actions impact more than just yourself—they affect those who look to you for guidance or inspiration.

For example, an NCAA athlete playing a pickup game may seem harmless, but the risk of injury or compromising eligibility outweighs the benefit. Similarly, as Christians, there are activities, conversations, or environments that, while not inherently sinful, may hinder our effectiveness or tarnish our witness. Romans 14:19 encourages us to pursue what leads to peace and mutual edification. Living a life on stage means choosing what is best over what is merely permissible, prioritizing God's purpose over personal preferences. By doing so, we avoid situations where our good intentions could be misinterpreted or misused.

Your Reputation Reflects Your Calling

Your reputation is not just about how others perceive you but how you represent Christ. Leaders, athletes, and influencers are held to higher standards because of their visibility. In 1 Timothy 3:2, Paul instructs leaders to be *"above reproach,"* meaning they should live in a way that avoids even the appearance of impropriety. This principle extends to anyone who represents Christ in the world.

Certain jokes, comments, or behaviors may seem trivial but can damage credibility. Even minor missteps can have outsized consequences in the age of screenshots and viral posts. Ephesians 4:29 encourages us, *"Do not let any unwholesome talk come out of your mouths, but only what helps build others up according to their needs."* Maintaining your influence requires constant vigilance, self-control, and a commitment to representing Christ well.

Maintaining Integrity on Stage

1. **Set Boundaries:** Be intentional about whom you associate with and what activities you engage in, understanding how they align with your calling.

2. **Use Discernment:** Think carefully before you speak, act, or post, ensuring that your choices reflect your values and glorify God.

3. **Remain Accountable:** Surround yourself with mentors or trusted friends who can provide guidance and hold you accountable in your walk.

4. **Pursue Peace:** Avoid unnecessary conflicts or actions that could lead others to misunderstand your intentions. Romans 14:19 reminds us to strive for what builds others up.

Living on stage is a privilege and responsibility. By guarding your associations, exercising discernment, and staying true to your values, you can maintain your influence and fulfill your calling, bringing glory to God in everything you do.

Affirmation Prayer

Heavenly Father,

Thank You for the privilege of influence and the calling You have placed on my life. Help me live with integrity and wisdom, understanding that my actions and words reflect myself and You. Teach me to discern what is helpful and what hinders my mission, guarding my heart against distractions or compromises.

Strengthen me to live a life that is above reproach, honoring You in my relationships, decisions, and interactions. May my life on stage point others to You and bring glory to Your name. Guide me to use my influence to build up, encourage, and inspire others to walk in Your truth.

In Jesus' name, Amen.

Chapter 18
The Production Stage

"Being confident of this, that He who began a good work in you will carry it on to completion until the day of Christ Jesus." (Philippians 1:6)

The production stage of your calling is the season when preparation transitions into action. It is when everything you've learned, endured, and developed converges, and God propels you into the fullness of your assignment. While stepping into your calling is exhilarating, it also demands boldness, unwavering faith, and continuous reliance on God's guidance. This stage is not the conclusion of your journey but the beginning of a lifetime of purpose, growth, and obedience.

Walking Boldly in Your Calling

Stepping into your calling requires courage and confidence. After years of preparation and trials, David finally became King of Israel in 2 Samuel 5. Though anointed as a young shepherd, David faced opposition from Saul, personal failures, and years of waiting before ascending to the throne. His journey teaches us that stepping into your calling often involves enduring challenges that refine your character and faith. When David became king, his first act was to inquire of the Lord, seeking divine guidance to defeat the Philistines (2 Samuel 5:19). David's boldness came from his trust in God's promises and his habit of seeking God's direction.

Similarly, Joshua stepped into his calling as the leader of Israel after the death of Moses. In Joshua 1:9, God encouraged him: *"Have I not commanded you? Be strong and courageous. Do not be afraid; do not be discouraged, for the Lord your God will be with you wherever you go."* Joshua's courage was rooted in God's presence and promises, allowing him to lead Israel into the Promised Land confidently. Like David and Joshua, we, too, must step into our calling with boldness, trusting that God has equipped and prepared us for the task ahead.

Paul's Instruction to Timothy

Paul's letters to Timothy provide valuable insights for anyone stepping into their calling. In 2 Timothy 4:2, Paul encourages Timothy: *"Preach the word; be prepared in and out of season; correct, rebuke, and encourage—with great patience and careful instruction."* This charge highlights the importance of readiness and persistence. Ministry and calling are not about convenience; they require faithfulness regardless of circumstances.

Paul also warns Timothy in 2 Timothy 1:6–7 to *"fan into flame the gift of God, which is in you through the laying on of my hands. The Spirit God gave us does not make us timid, but gives us power, love, and self-discipline."* The gifts and calling of God require nurturing. Just as a fire needs tending to remain strong, we must continually stir up the gifts within us through prayer, study, and action. Paul's instructions remind us that stepping into our calling is an ongoing process of growth, endurance, and reliance on God's Spirit.

Continuing to Seek God's Guidance

The production stage is not a time to rely solely on past preparation or human wisdom. Like David and Joshua, we must remain dependent on God's guidance. Proverbs 3:5–6 instructs, *"Trust in the Lord with all your heart and lean not on your understanding; in all your ways submit to Him, and He will make your paths straight."* This dependence keeps us aligned with His will, ensuring we do not stray from the path He has set before us.

Paul's reminder to Timothy to rightly handle the Word of God (2 Timothy 2:15) also applies to us. Whether our calling involves preaching, leading, or serving, we must continually seek God's wisdom and direction through prayer and study. The production stage is not about self-reliance but about walking in step with the Holy Spirit, allowing Him to guide every decision and action.

This Is Only the Beginning

It is crucial to remember that stepping into your calling is not the end of the journey but the start of a lifelong mission. Philippians 1:6 assures us that God, who began the good work in us, will carry it to completion. Each step in the production stage prepares us for greater levels of growth and responsibility.

David and Joshua faced battles after stepping into their roles, and Timothy had to confront false teachings and challenges in the church. Similarly, your calling will involve highs and lows, victories and struggles. But as Paul reminds us in Galatians 6:9, *"Let us not grow weary in doing good, for at the proper time we will reap a harvest if we do not give up."* The production stage is about perseverance and trusting God to complete the work He has started.

The production stage is a time to walk boldly, seek God continually, and embrace the journey with faith and confidence. It is the start of a lifetime of impact, as God uses you to carry out His plans for His glory. Following the examples of David, Joshua, and Paul's instructions to Timothy, we can follow our calling with courage and steadfastness, trusting that God is faithful to complete the work He has started in us.

Affirmation Prayer

Heavenly Father,

Thank You for calling me and for your work in my life. As I step into this new season, help me to walk boldly, trusting in Your promises and guidance. Teach me to seek You continually and rely on Your wisdom and strength. I declare that this is not the end but the beginning of a lifetime of fulfilling Your purpose.

Strengthen my heart to persevere through challenges, and remind me that You, who began this good work, will complete it. I surrender this stage to You, confident that You will guide my steps and equip me to fulfill all You have called me to do.

In Jesus' name, Amen.

Chapter 19
Faithful to the Call

Key Verse: "Be faithful, even to the point of death, and I will give you life as your victor's crown." (Revelation 2:10)

Faithfulness to the call of God is not a suggestion but a command, central to fulfilling His purpose for your life. To be faithful means to be steadfast, reliable, and unwavering in God's task. The Greek word for faithful πιστός (*pistos*) conveys trustworthiness and loyalty. This faithfulness is not about perfection but persistence—remaining committed to the calling regardless of challenges. God's call comes with His assurance that He will provide the strength, grace, and resources you need to succeed. I will never forget what god said years ago, *"I will energize what I authorized."* God will empower you to fulfill the assignment if God has called you.

Faithful Even Unto Death

Revelation 2:10 encourages believers to remain faithful even to the point of death, promising the crown of life as a reward. This level of faithfulness requires deep trust in God's sovereignty and the eternal value of His calling. Biblical figures like Stephen exemplified unwavering commitment. In Acts 7, Stephen boldly proclaimed the gospel despite facing martyrdom. Even in the face of death, his faithfulness reminds us that God's call is worth every sacrifice because it leads to eternal reward.

Jesus modeled ultimate faithfulness, obediently fulfilling His mission to the cross (Philippians 2:8). He trusted the Father's plan, knowing His sacrifice would bring redemption to humanity. Faithfulness may not always mean physical martyrdom, but it does require dying to ourselves—our fears, desires, and ambitions—so that Christ's purpose can be fulfilled in us. Faithfulness means trusting that God's plan is more significant than anything we could imagine, even when the path is difficult.

Now That You See the Process

Faithfulness to the call often involves preparation, testing, and refinement. Understanding this process helps you navigate challenges while maintaining sight of your purpose. Consider Joseph, who endured betrayal, false accusations, and imprisonment before stepping into his purpose. Now that you see the process, you won't be caught off guard when trials come. James 1:3–4 reminds us, *"Because you know that the testing of your faith produces perseverance. Let perseverance finish its work so you may be mature and complete, not lacking anything."* Every step, whether joyful or painful, is part of God's preparation for the next stage of your calling.

God Called You to Succeed

One of the most important truths to remember is that God does not call you to fail. If He called you, He has already equipped you to succeed. Philippians 1:6 declares, *"Being confident of this, that He who began a good work in you will carry it on to completion until the day of Christ*

Jesus." Your success in fulfilling your calling is not about your abilities but about God's power working through you. Moses doubted his ability to lead Israel, but God assured him in Exodus 3:12, *"I will be with you."* That same promise applies to you today.

The phrase *"God will energize what He authorized"* reminds us that God provides the resources, strength, and grace needed to complete the assignment He has given. Your calling comes with divine backing, and as you step out in faith, God's power will meet you at every step. Your faithfulness activates His provision, and He will finish what He started in you.

Being Instant In Season and Out of Season

Paul's instruction to Timothy in 2 Timothy 4:2, *"Preach the word; be prepared in season and out of season,"* speaks to the need for faithfulness in all circumstances. Being "in season" refers to times when ministry feels fruitful and supported, while "out of season" points to times of difficulty or opposition. Faithfulness requires persistence in both, knowing that God's call is unchanging even when the season shifts.

This faithfulness requires spiritual readiness, like the wise virgins in Matthew 25:1–13 who kept their lamps filled with oil. Keeping your spiritual "lamp" full means staying connected to God through prayer, worship, and the Word, ensuring you are always prepared to fulfill His purpose.

Encouraging Others Along the Way

Faithfulness to the call also involves building up others. Hebrews 10:24 says, *"And let us consider how we may spur one another on toward love and good deeds."* Just as Barnabas encouraged Paul and John Mark in their ministries, we are called to uplift and inspire others to remain faithful to their callings. Encouragement strengthens the body of Christ and reminds us that we are not alone in this journey.

Study to Show Yourself Approved

Paul's instruction in 2 Timothy 2:15, *"Study to show yourself approved unto God, a workman that needeth not to be ashamed,"* underscores the importance of preparation. Faithfulness to the call requires intentionality in studying God's Word and applying it to your life. Diligence ensures you can handle challenges, discern truth, and fulfill your assignment excellently.

This Is Only the Beginning

Faithfulness to the call is not a one-time decision but a lifetime commitment. Philippians 1:6 reminds us that God, who began the good work in us, will carry it to completion. Each step in our journey is part of a larger story that God is writing. Walking faithfully in your calling means embracing the process, trusting God through every season, and relying on Him for strength and guidance.

Faithfulness to the call is a walk of obedience, endurance, and trust. As you remain steadfast, you honor God and fulfill the purpose for which you were created, leaving a legacy of faith and impact that echoes into eternity.

Affirmation Prayer

Heavenly Father,

Thank You for calling me and equipping me for the purpose You have placed in my life. Help me be faithful in every season, trusting You through challenges and victories. Now that I understand the process, I have strengthened my heart to remain steadfast and not be caught off guard. Remind me that You have called me to succeed and that I can fulfill every part of my assignment with You.

May I walk with boldness, diligence, and humility, trusting that You will energize what You have authorized. Teach me to encourage others along the way and be ready every season to carry out Your will. I surrender my life and call to You, knowing You are faithful.

In Jesus' name, Amen.

Chapter 20
Congratulations

Key Verse: "But you will receive power when the Holy Spirit comes on you, and you will be my witnesses in Jerusalem, and in all Judea and Samaria, and to the ends of the earth." (Acts 1:8)

Congratulations! Reaching this point in the journey is no small accomplishment. Your determination, faith, and willingness to grow in your calling demonstrate the depth of your commitment to God's purpose for your life. The fact that you are still here, reading, reflecting, and pressing forward, is evidence of your desire to fulfill the mission God has placed within you. As Dr. Mike Murdock wisely said, *"The proof of desire is pursuit."* By pursuing this journey, you have shown your hunger for more of God and your willingness to act on it.

Years ago, the Lord spoke a powerful word to me: *"You are sent to deliver the deliverers."* If you are reading this, I want you to know that you are one of those deliverers. God has placed His Spirit within you, not just to transform your own life but to empower you to impact the lives of others. Acts 1:8 speaks directly to your calling: *"You will receive power when the Holy Spirit comes on you, and you will be my witnesses."* This power is not just for personal victories but for advancing God's kingdom on earth. You have been chosen as His agent, a carrier of His love, truth, and deliverance to a world in need.

As a deliverer, your calling is not dependent on outsider approval. You have nothing to prove to anyone but God. Your value, purpose, and identity are rooted in Him alone. Isaiah 43:1 reminds us, *"Do not fear, for I have redeemed you; I have summoned you by name; you are mine."* God has handpicked, equipped, and positioned you for this time. You are not a mistake or an afterthought; you are chosen, called, and sent.

Sometimes, walking in your calling will make you look crazy to others. Obedience to God often defies human logic and societal norms, but trust that what seems foolish now will make sense in time. Consider Noah, who spent decades building an ark on dry land based solely on God's command. People mocked him, doubted his sanity, and questioned his actions, but Noah remained faithful. Ultimately, his obedience saved his family and preserved the future of humanity (Genesis 6:13–22). You, too, may face criticism, doubt, or even isolation as you pursue what God has called you to do. But remember, what looks like faithfulness to God may look like foolishness to the world. Stay the course because the reward of your obedience will far outweigh the ridicule. What seems crazy now will make perfect sense when God's promises are fulfilled in your life.

Remember, as God's agent on earth, your mission is not about perfection but obedience. It is about walking in the authority and power He has given you through His Spirit. Your journey so far proves you are capable, resilient, and faithful to the call. God doesn't make mistakes, and He doesn't choose people at random. He has seen your potential and declared you fit for His service.

As you continue this journey, hold fast to this truth: you are not alone. The God who called you will sustain you. Philippians 1:6 promises, *"Being confident of this, that He who began a good work in you will carry it on to completion until the day of Christ Jesus."* Your calling is secure in Him, and your obedience will bear fruit for His glory.

You are called to stand out, not to blend in—you are the difference. God has set you apart to be a light in the darkness, a city on a hill that cannot be hidden (Matthew 5:14). Your calling is unique, and your obedience to it is critical for fulfilling God's purpose. Do not be ashamed of who you are or what God has called you to do. When I founded Victory City Church, I had to stick with God's vision, even when it didn't look like what others were doing. There were moments when I felt pressured to conform, but I knew that obedience to God mattered more than approval from people. Following His vision required courage and faith, but it was worth it because it was His plan, not mine.

In this journey, you must be cautious about who you take advice from. Don't seek direction from people who haven't advanced in the areas you're called to go. They may mean well, but their advice can derail you if it doesn't align with God's word. Proverbs 13:20 reminds us, *"Walk with the wise and become wise, for a companion of fools suffers harm."* Surround yourself with people who inspire you to grow, challenge you to stay faithful to God's vision, and have a track record of obedience and success in their walk with Him. Remember, you were not created to follow the crowd but to lead with purpose, confidence, and boldness in your divine assignment.

You've come this far because God has chosen, equipped, and called you for a purpose greater than yourself. Your journey is just beginning, and the impact of your faithfulness will ripple through lives and generations. Stand tall, knowing that you are a deliverer, sent by God to bring light and hope to the world.

Affirmation Prayer

Heavenly Father,

Thank You for choosing me and equipping me for Your purpose. I recognize that I am not just called but also empowered by Your Spirit to be a deliverer, a witness of Your love and truth in the earth. Strengthen me to walk boldly in my calling, knowing I have nothing to prove to anyone but You.

Help me remain faithful, obedient, and focused on your mission. I surrender every fear, doubt, and insecurity, trusting that You have prepared the way. Thank You for the privilege of being Your agent on earth and carrying Your message of hope and freedom to those in need.

In Jesus' name, Amen.

Made in the USA
Columbia, SC
26 December 2024